# Popular Titles
# and Subtitles of
# MUSICAL COMPOSITIONS

### Second Edition

by

FREDA PASTOR BERKOWITZ

The Scarecrow Press, Inc.

Metuchen, N. J.     1975

Library of Congress Cataloging in Publication Data

Berkowitz, Freda Pastor.
    Popular titles and subtitles of musical compositions.

    Bibliography: p.
    Includes index.
    1.   Titles of musical compositions--Bibliography.
2.   Music--Bibliography.   I.   Title.
ML113. B39    1975          016. 78           75-4751
ISBN 0-8108-0806-4

To My Grandsons
GREGORY, PETER and HANS

# INTRODUCTION

For more than three hundred years, composers of serious music have used a relatively small number of general titles for their compositions. There are tens of thousands of works called "Sonata," "Symphony," "String Quartet" and so on; and even though composers have defined their works more specifically by adding the key and the opus number, as in "Sonata in A, op. 58," there remained the desire on the part of publishers, performers, and listeners, for a literary label which would make it easier to identify the composition, and would give a clue to the mood of the piece, or at least to a significant characteristic.

Nicknames and sometimes subtitles are a peculiar appendage to the art of music. Strangely enough, they usually were added by publishers, editors, critics, friends (or enemies) of the composer--seldom by the composer himself. Often the origins of these unofficial appellations are shrouded in mystery or are based on legends or conjectures that have almost become legends.

The aim of this present volume is to offer a collection of these nicknames and subtitles which have become associated with works from 1600 up until the present time. These will be listed in English, as well as in the original language, together with some information regarding their origins whenever possible. There will undoubtedly be some omissions but all those included are traceable to biographical and historical sources.

In order to permit the precise identification of compositions by composers for whom thematic catalogues have been published, reference is made to these works, using the standard abbreviations for them, in parentheses following the formal title. The full title of these catalogues will be found in the bibliography.

I want to thank my friends, particularly Dr. Otto E.

v

Albrecht, Professor Emeritus of Music and Curator of the Albrecht Music Library of the University of Pennsylvania, for his encouragement and great help all during the time I was revising this book.

I owe particular gratitude to Mr. Ralph Berkowitz for his many valuable suggestions, to Mr. Edward N. Waters, Chief of the Music Division of the Library of Congress, Washington D. C., for his great cooperation and patience in answering all my questions; to the wonderful staff at the library of the Curtis Institute of Music, particularly Mr. Gordon Mapes, for their willingness to help me find information; to Miss Elizabeth R. Hartman of The Free Library of Philadelphia for assisting me in finding the necessary reference material; to the many composers for so graciously giving me information about their compositions; to Mr. H. C. Robbins Landon for his valuable Haydn information; to Mr. John N. Burk for his help on Mozart and Beethoven; to Miss Dika Newlin for her enlightening remarks on the music of Bruckner and Mahler; to Mr. James W. Keeler, Vice President of Creative Programming for Radio Station WFLN in Philadelphia for permitting me to examine the record covers of many albums.

ABBREVIATIONS

| arr | arranged by | no. | number |
|---|---|---|---|
| attrib | attributed | op. | opus (opera) |
| movt | movement | | |

Freda Pastor Berkowitz

# THEMATIC CATALOGUES
Referred to in the Text

Brown         Maurice J. E. Brown. Chopin; An Index of His Works in Chronological Order. 2nd ed. London: Macmillan, 1972.

Burghauser     Jarmil Burghauser. Antonín Dvořák; Thematic Catalogue, Bibliography, Survey of His Life and Work. Praha, 1967.

Cauchie        Maurice Cauchie. Thematic Index of the Works of François Couperin. Monaco: Lyrebird Press, 1949.

D.              Otto Erich Deutsch. Schubert; Thematic Catalogue of All His Works. London: J. M. Dent & Sons, 1951.

Gérard         Yves Gérard. Thematic, Bibliographical and Critical Catalogue of the Works of Boccherini. London: Oxford University Press, 1969.

Hob.           Anthony van Hoboken. Joseph Haydn: Thematisch-bibliographisches Werkverzeichnis. Mainz: B. Schotts Söhne, 1957- .

Hopkinson     Cecil Hopkinson. A Bibliographical Thematic Catalogue of the Works of John Field. London, 1961.

F.              Istituto Italiano Antonio Vivaldi. Antonio Vivaldi, Catalogo Numerico-Tematico delle Opere Strumentali. Milano: Edizioni Ricordi, 1968. (Numbers refer to the classification of Antonio Fanna.)

WoO          Georg Kinsky. Das Werk Beethovens. The-

matisch-bibliographisches Verzeichnis seiner
sämtlichen vollendeten Kompositionen.
München: G. Henle, 1955. (WoO is "Werke
ohne Opuszahl, " works without opus no. )

K.     Ralph Kirkpatrick. Domenico Scarlatti.
       Princeton, N. J. : Princeton University
       Press, 1953.

K.     Ludwig, Ritter von Köchel. Chronologisch-
       thematisches Verzeichnis sämtlicher Ton-
       werke Wolfgang Amadé Mozarts. 6th ed.
       Wiesbaden: Breitkopf und Härtel, [1964].

L.     Alessandro Longo, ed. Domenico Scarlatti.
       Opere Complete per clavicembalo. 10 vols.,
       supplement and thematic index. Milano:
       Ricordi, 1947-51.

BWV    Wolfgang Schmieder. Thematisch-systemati-
       sches Verzeichnis der musikalischen Werke
       von Johann Sebastian Bach. Leipzig: Breit-
       kopf und Härtel, 1950. (Bach Werk-Ver-
       zeichnis. )

Wotquenne   Alfred Wotquenne, ed. Thematisches Ver-
            zeichnis der Werke von Carl Philipp
            Emanuel Bach. Leipzig: Breitkopf und
            Härtel, 1905.

Zimmerman   Franklin B. Zimmerman. Henry Purcell,
            1659-1695: An Analytical Catalogue of
            His Music. London: Macmillan, 1963.

# POPULAR TITLES AND SUBTITLES*

1 "Academic Festival Overture"
   Brahms. Overture in C minor, op. 80

   In the spring of 1879, the University of Breslau conferred upon Brahms an honorary doctorate of philosophy, naming him in its diploma "Artis Musicae severioris in Germania nunc princeps" [now the foremost exponent in Germany of musical life in the more severe style]. For what he termed his doctor's thesis, Brahms wrote the "Academic Festival Overture," a jolly pot-pourri on student songs "à la Suppé," as he jokingly called it.

2 "Adelaide Concerto"
   Mozart. Concerto for Violin in D major (K. Anhang C. 14. 05)

   The enigma of the so-called "Adelaide Concerto" is still unsolved. This was published by Marius Casadesus in 1933 with the suggestion that it was composed by Mozart at Versailles at the age of 10 for the use of the eldest daughter of Louis XIV, Princess Adelaide, to whom the manuscript is dedicated. This manuscript, which is in a private collection in France, is on only two staves, giving merely the solo part and a line of bass with occasional fragmentary hints of the other parts. The remainder of the published score is the work of Casadesus himself. Unfortunately neither he nor Alfred Einstein, the Mozart expert, was permitted to see the manuscript. However, it is well known that Mozart often wrote down the first draft of a composition in the form of a short score, so that is not surprising. But the surprising feature is the date, which according to the foreword of Schotts Sohne edition is May 26, 1766. Alfred Einstein has the fol-

---

*Full names and vital dates of composers are given in the Composer Index, at the end of the book.

1

lowing objections to the date:   Mozart was not at Versailles
at the date on the autograph; and in 1768, two years after
the date given on the manuscript, Mozart's father made a
catalogue of the works of the boy and this was not included.
    "If perhaps someday it is established that the short
score is a genuine autograph, one would have at least a work
which considerably enriches our knowledge of Mozart's first
steps in that form" [Friedrich Blume, in Landon, The Mozart
Companion, p. 220].


3    "Adieu à Guillaume Kolberg"
     Chopin.   Polonaise for Piano in Bb major (Brown 13)

    According to footnotes in the Breitkopf und Härtel edition
of this work, the Bb minor Polonaise dates from the days
just preceding Chopin's departure for Bad Reinertz in 1826
with his mother and sisters.   Both Chopin and his sister,
Emilya, had been ill and their mother was taking them to the
spa in Prussian Silesia for a summer rest cure.
    Shortly before leaving, Chopin was graduated from the
Lyceum, and to celebrate the event he and his schoolmate,
Wilhelm Kolberg, attended a performance of Rossini's opera,
La Gazza Ladra.   When they parted, Chopin presented Wilhelm with this polonaise, in which he had inscribed, "Adieu
à Guillaume Kolberg."


4    "L'Adieu à Varsovie" [Farewell to Warsaw]
     Chopin.   Rondo in C minor, op. 1   (Brown 10)


5    "L'Adieu Valse"
     Chopin.   Waltz for Piano, op. 69 no. 1, in Ab major
     (Brown 95)

    During the summer of 1835 Chopin visited his friends,
the Wodzinskis, in Dresden.   There he met Marya, their
young attractive daughter of 19, and fell passionately in love
with her.   At first Marya's mother approved of their friendship, but later, influenced by her husband who thought it a
bad match, insisted that the relationship between the young
people be severed.   As a parting gift Chopin presented Marya
with this waltz in Ab major either on September 23 or 24,
1835 and added the word "L'Adieu" to the autograph.

6    "Les Adieux" (or, "Les Adieux, L'Absence et Le Retour")
Beethoven.    Sonata [No. 26] for Piano in E♭ major, op.
81A

At the age of 16 the Archduke Rudolph had become a
great friend and favorite pupil of Beethoven.    The composer
dedicated many important works to him during their friendship.
When this sonata was written Archduke Rudolph and
the rest of the royal family were forced to leave Vienna because the city was being attacked by Napoleon's forces.    Beethoven was greatly upset because of this and the piece is a
veritable monument to the friendship the composer felt for
the Archduke.    In Beethoven's sketches, which he kept just
for himself, were the words, "as written from the heart and
dedicated to H. R. H. "    The three movements of the sonata
deal with the emotions of "Parting, " "Absence" and "Return. "

7    "Adventures on the Edge of a Precipice"
Arnold Bax.    Symphony No. 1

A symphony in three movements, the first of which is
responsible for the subtitle:    1. Adventures on the Edge of
a Precipice; 2. Centuries in the Abyss; 3. A Successful Rock
Climb.

8    "Aeolian Harp"
Chopin.    Etude for Piano, op. 25 no. 1, in A♭ major
(Brown 104)

It is very possible that the following comment of Robert
Schumann concerning Chopin's playing of this etude had something to do with the nickname, "Aeolian Harp": "Imagine an
Aeolian harp having all the scales, and an artist's hand com-
bining them with all kinds of fantastic embellishments but always with an audible deeper tone in the basses and a softly
flowing cantilena in the treble--and you will have some idea
of his playing.    No wonder then that we were charmed most
of all by those pieces which we had heard him play and especially by the first, in A♭ major, more a poem than a
study" [quoted in Weinstock, Chopin, p. 212].
Many times this etude is referred to as the "Shepherd
Boy Etude. "    Chopin is supposed to have told a pupil that
when he was writing the piece he had imagined a little shepherd taking refuge in a grotto during a storm and to make the
time pass more pleasantly he played a melody on his flute.

9  "Africa"
   Saint-Saëns.   Fantasie for Piano and Orchestra, op. 89,
   in G minor

   In the winter of 1891, Saint-Saëns went to Ceylon and
during the trip home spent some time in Cairo, Egypt, where
the Fantasie "Africa" was composed.  He tried to portray the
scene of the native music ushering in a night of religious rev-
els in an African village.  The instrumentation suggests the
tom-tom sounds that the native musicians produced from their
gourd and skin drums.

10  "Agitation"  (see "Songs Without Words")
    Mendelssohn.   Piece for Piano, op. 53 no. 3, in G
    minor

11  "Air on the G String"
    J. S. Bach (arr by Wilhelmi).   Air from Suite in D
    major (3d movt)  (BWV 1068)

   August Daniel Ferdinand Victor Wilhelmi (1845-1908), a
famous violinist and teacher, composed and arranged various
pieces for the violin.  Among these arrangements is the well
known "Air on the G String," which he took from the third
movement of this Overture or Suite in D major.

12  "Alassio"  (see "In the South")
    Elgar.   Overture, op. 50

13  "Alla Rustica"
    Vivaldi.   Concerto for Harpsichord and Strings in G
    major  (F. XI, 11)

14  "Alla Turca"
    Mozart.   Sonata for Piano in A major (3d movt)  (K.
    331)

   It is the Rondo movement of this sonata which has given
it its nickname.  The movement is gay and amusing and
points the way to the exotic "Turkish Music" that is found
in "Die Entführung."
   John N. Burk, Mozart and His Music, said, "This one
is an applause catcher as plainly designed for a general audience as some of his party music--as usual, when Mozart becomes deliberately 'popular' he is quite irresistible" [p. 375].

15  "Alleluia"
    Haydn.   Symphony No. 30 in C major   (Hob. I, 30)

The idea of using church melodies in secular compositions seems to have fascinated Haydn.   When he composed
his Symphony No. 30, in 1765, he based the first movement
on an original Gregorian melody.   The melody turned out to
be the old Alleluia sung during Holy Week, and the symphony
was appropriately subtitled "Alleluia. "   The first movement
was originally intended for performance on Easter morning.


16  "Altitudes"
    Jean Martinon.   Symphony No. 4, op. 53

As the subtitle suggests, the Fourth Symphony was inspired by Alpine mountain climbing.   The composer has
written the following on the flyleaf of his score, "For what
do they reach, these climbers of mountains?   Like the pioneers of Cosmos, they seek the presence of God, God!
The purest and most formidable work that mankind has ever
invented. "


17  "Amaranth"
    Harold Morris.   Symphony No. 3

The composer subtitled his Third Symphony "Amaranth"
because he wrote it after reading the poem of Edwin Arling-
ton Robinson, by that title.   However, the symphony is not
connected with the poem in subject matter.   Amaranth means
a flower which never fades.


18  "American Quartet"
    Dvořák.   String Quartet No. 6 [new no. 12] in F major,
       op. 96   (Burghauser 179)

This work was written in Spillville, Iowa, in 1893 and
like others of the composer's works of the American period
uses some thematic material with characteristics found in
Negro songs (e. g. , pentatonic scales, syncopation).   In the
United States it is called the "American Quartet. "   In England it has been called the "Nigger Quartet. "   The first
performance was given by the Kneisel Quartet in Boston on
January 1, 1894.

19  "An American Sketch"
Gottschalk.  Le Banjo, op. 15, for Piano

Robert Offergeld has pointed out that this "Banjo" was
the second one that Louis Moreau Gottschalk composed.  As
he dedicated it to the "Firemen of New Orleans," introducing
popular airs and imitations of the banjo and firebells, it was
subtitled "An American Sketch. "

20  "L'Amoroso" [the lover]
Vivaldi.  Concerto for Violin, Strings and Harpsichord
in E major  (F. I, 127)

21  "Andante Favori"
Beethoven.  Andante in F major for Piano  (WoO 57)

The Andante in F major was composed in the years
1803-1804 as a slow movement for the "Waldstein Sonata"
(q. v.), Op. 53.  A friend of Beethoven suggested that the
movement was too long for the sonata and that he write a
shorter one.  Beethoven's first reaction was one of anger,
but after giving it some thought he did follow the suggestion
and in the words of Egon Kenton, "as a mother would com-
pensate a criticized child, placed the slighted Andante alone
and it was published as 'Andante Favori'. "

22  "Angel of Death"
Josef Suk.  Symphony, op. 27, in C minor  (Asrael)

The composer had started writing this symphony as a
memorial to his father-in-law, Antonin Dvořák.  Unfortunately, by the time he had finished the third movement a year
later (1905) his wife had also died.  The music is filled
with bitterness and struggle against Fate and Death and it
is because of this that the composer subtitled his symphony,
"Angel of Death. "

23  "Angels' Serenade"
Gaetano Braga.  Leggenda Valacca, Piece for Cello and
Piano

Braga was an Italian cellist and composer who wrote

this little cello piece and named it "Leggenda Valacca. "
However, its great popularity was achieved under the nickname, "Angels' Serenade. " It has been arranged for various instrumental combinations, as a piano solo, and also as
a vocal solo.


24   "Antar"
     Rimsky-Korsakov.   Symphony no. 2, op. 9 (later,
     "Oriental Suite")

     Rimsky-Korsakov was inspired to write his second sym-
phony which he subtitled "Antar, " after reading a story
written by Sennkowsky, of which Antar was the hero.   Antar was a famous warrior-poet who lived in the sixth century.   His eloquence and inspiration as a poet were so
revered that one of his poems, inscribed upon deerskin, was
hung up among the idols of the Kaaba at Mecca for the
adoration of worshippers.


25   "Antartica" [sic]
     Vaughan Williams.   Symphony No. 7

     The Symphony No. 7 had its origin in an earlier work
which Ralph Vaughan Williams had written for the film
"Scott of the Antarctic. " It is the eerie use of a wind ma-
chine, the effect of a hidden choir of women's voices and
the brittle sounds of the vibraphone, xylophone, celeste,
piano and glockenspiel that give the feeling of the icy Antarctic landscape.


26   "Apocalyptic" (see "The German Michel")
     Bruckner.   Symphony No. 8 in C minor

     It is undoubtedly the title of the last movement of this
symphony, "An Apocalyptic Vision of the Cosmos at the
Last Day, " that has given the symphony its nickname.   The
unlimited thematic richness of the Finale shows that Bruckner gave more of his soul in this music than in any other
preceding work.
     In the last movement, at a point when the themes of
all four movements enter simultaneously, the autograph has
the exclamation "Halleluja. "

27   "Appassionata"
     Beethoven.   Sonata for Piano, op. 57, in F minor

     This subtitle was given to the work by the publisher
Cranz, of Hamburg, in the four-hand arrangement published
in 1838.
     Sir Donald Francis Tovey, in his A Companion to
Beethoven's Pianoforte Sonatas, writes the following concerning the subtitle:  "It is justified by the eminently tragic tone
of the whole work.   No other work of Beethoven maintains
a tragic solemnity throughout all its movements....   In the
'Sonata Appassionata' the very beginning of the Finale is in
itself a final stroke of fate, after which there is not a
moment's doubt that the tragic passion is rushing death-
wards" [p. 177].


28   "Appassionata"   (see "Songs Without Words")
     Mendelssohn.   Piece for Piano, op. 38 no. 5, in A
       minor


29   "Apponyi Quartets"
     Haydn.   String Quartets, op. 71 (3)  (Hob. III, 69-71);
       and String Quartets, op. 74 (3)  (Hob. III, 72-74)

     According to the autographs preserved in the state li-
brary of Berlin, Haydn composed these six string quartets
in 1793.   They were published as Op. 71 and 74, listed as
follows:  op. 71 no. 1 in B♭ major; op. 71 no. 2 in D
major; op. 71 no. 3 in E♭ major; op. 74 no. 1 in C major; op. 74 no. 2 in F major; op. 74 no. 3 in G minor.
     Haydn wrote them at a time when he was very much
interested in orchestral composition and they show a certain
orchestral quality.   For the first time the composer wrote
introductions to the first movements, a feature that played
an important part in his symphonies.   The quartets were
written for and dedicated to Count Apponyi.


30   "Archduke Trio"
     Beethoven.   Trio for Piano and Strings, op. 97, in B♭
       major.

     In Beethoven's sketch book of 1810 there are evidences
of this trio.   However, it was not until March 1811, and
then within a period of three weeks, that the trio was

written.   The work was not published until 1816, with a
dedication to Beethoven's patron and pupil, Archduke Rudolph
of Austria, hence the nickname.
It is said that at the time the Trio was written there
was no copyist available and the Archduke was so anxious to
perform the piece that he played it directly from the autograph.

31   "The Ardeatine Caves"
William Schuman.   Symphony No. 9

In Schuman's notes to his Symphony No. 9 he says the
following:   "In none of my previous symphonies have I used
an extrinsic or non-musical program element.   Therefore
I would like first to attempt an explanation of why I have
done so in Symphony No. 9.   Precisely what is the relationship of the subtitle, the Ardeatine Caves, to the music?   It
was inspired by two visits to the Ardeatine Caves in Rome.
And although the work does not attempt to depict the horror
of what I saw realistically, I chose the subtitle for philosophical reasons. "

32   "Ariadne's Lament"
Pietro Locatelli.   Concerto Grosso, op. 7 no. 6

33   "Arjuna"
Hovhaness.   Symphony No. 8, op. 100

34   "Arpeggione"
Schubert.   Sonata for Cello and Piano in A minor   (D.
821)

Schubert wrote this sonata for the arpeggione, a cello-
like stringed instrument.   The life of the instrument was
brief and the only reason that it is remembered is because
of the sonata Schubert wrote.   It is now played on the cello
with piano accompaniment.

35   "Au Tombeau"
Pietro Locatelli.   Sonata in F major for Violin and
Piano, op. 6 no. 5

36   "Auferstehung"   (see "Resurrection")
     Mahler.   Symphony No. 2 in C minor


37   "Aus Meinem Leben"   (see "From My Life")
     Bedřich Smetana.   String Quartet No. 1 in E minor


38   "The Aviary" [L'Uccelliera]
     Luigi Boccherini.   Quintet No. 12 for two Violins, Viola
     and two Cellos in D major, op. 11 no. 6   (Gérard
     276)

     According to Gérard, "the subtitle 'The Aviary' is re-
corded by Boccherini himself and the descriptive character
of this quintet is evident.   It is clear that the inspiration
for these musical scenes, typical of the taste of the period
for 'les bergeries,' came to the composer from the collection of birds which was brought together and beautifully
cared for in the aviaries of the Infante Don Luis and from
the tapestries of the hunt which decorated the royal apart-
ments of his master. "


39   "Babi Yar"
     Shostakovich.   Symphony No. 13

     This Symphony No. 13 is so subtitled because the first
of the five movements is called "Babi Yar. "   This is music
written to the text by the outspoken poet Yevgeny Yevtushen-
ko, which produced a great deal of criticism in Moscow.
The symphony was banned and remained hidden until the
initial Western Hemisphere performances were given in
Philadelphia and New York City in January 1970 [from Philadelphia Orchestra Program Notes, January 1970, p. 19].


40   "The Bagpipes"
     Haydn.   (Russian) Dance No. 16   (Hob. XIX, 4)

     This is one of a set of pieces Haydn wrote for musical
clocks.   Niemecz, Prince Esterházy's librarian, built these
clocks and in them used music written by his friend and
teacher, Joseph Haydn.   The latter presented one of these
musical clocks to the Austrian court conductor, Florian
Gassmann, and the music it played was a Russian Dance
which the Gassmann family nicknamed "The Bagpipes. "

41  "Balm Study"
    Chopin.  Etude for Piano, op. 25 no. 2, in F minor
    (Brown 97)


42  "Le Banquet Infernal"
    Chopin.  Scherzo for Piano No. 1, op. 20, in B minor
    (Brown 65)

This scherzo has been so called perhaps because of its
wild power and grandeur.  In fact all four scherzos stand
on a pedestal all of their own; they are indeed no "jokes"
("scherzos") in any sense.


43  "Barcarolle"
    Scarlatti.  Sonata for Piano  (L. 132, K. 429)


44  "Basler Concerto"
    Stravinsky.  Concerto in D major for Strings

Nicolas Slonimsky [Music Since 1900, p. 588] has explained that when the Basel chamber orchestra had its 20th
anniversary its conductor, Paul Sacher, commissioned
Stravinsky to write a new work to commemorate the event.
The result was a chamber concerto modelled after the
classical concerto grosso.  It was introduced in Basel,
Switzerland, on January 21, 1947, and has since been known
as the "Basler Concerto."


45  "La Bataille"  (see "The Battle")
    Mozart.  Contretanz for Orchestra  (K. 535)


46  "The Battle" [La Bataille]
    Mozart.  Contretanz for Orchestra  (K. 535)

In Köchel's thematic catalog the author says that there
is no definite reason why this particular nickname was given
to this contretanz.  Actually Lausch refers to it in the
Wiener Zeitung of March 19, 1788 as the "Siege of Belgrade."  However, there is somewhat of a discrepancy in
this statement because Belgrade was not conquered until
September 7, 1789, by General Laudon.  But war had indeed
been declared in February 1788 and the Austrians were
counting on a prompt attack on the Turks.

47   "The Battle of Vittoria" [Wellington's Victory]
     Beethoven.  Symphony for Orchestra, op. 91

     Mälzel was an inventor and friend of Beethoven.  His
newly perfected "Panharmonicon" was a mechanical brass
band all contained in a single case.  The instruments were
blown through a bellows and their notes controlled by a revolving brass cylinder with pins.
     Besides being an inventor, Mälzel was also a clever
business man and when the news of Wellington's victory at
Vittoria, June 21, 1813, reached Vienna, he conceived the
idea of a "Battle Piece" especially written by Beethoven
for the Panharmonicon.  The composer was docile for once
and he allowed his intended partner to plan the musical
scheme.  To appeal to the English public, the tune of "Rule
Britannia" and a fugue on "God Save The King" were part
of the new work, which was dedicated to the English Prince
Regent, the future King George IV.  The original plan was
to exhibit the huge instrument in England with the "Battle
Piece" and, if possible, to exhibit the composer too.  However, this scheme did not work out because neither Mälzel
nor Beethoven had funds for such a venture.
     Beethoven rewrote the symphony for full orchestra
and Mälzel arranged a charity concert for its performance.
Distinguished musicians were so amused at this unabashed
"Battle Piece" that they willingly offered their services to
play.  Very soon after the first successful performance, a
paid concert was arranged for the newly composed Symphony
No. 7 in A major and "The Battle of Vittoria."  The former
was much applauded, the allegretto had to be repeated, but
the latter created a sensation.


48   "The Bear" [L'Ours]
     Haydn.  Symphony No. 82 in C major  (Hob. I, 82)

     According to the testimony of the autograph, the Sym-
phony No. 82 was actually the first Paris Symphony of the
set of six (82 through 87) which Haydn was commissioned to
write for the fashionable Parisian concert series "La Loge
Olympique."  The nickname originates from the last movement with its gruff but cheerful growls of bass pedal-points,
sometimes referred to as the "Bear" or "Bagpipe" dance.


49   "The Bee's Wedding"  (see "Spinning Song")
     Mendelssohn.  No. 34 from "Songs Without Words" for
        Piano, op. 67 no. 4

50    "The Bell"   (see "Quinten")
      Haydn.   String Quartet, op. 76 no. 2, in D minor
       (Hob. III, 76)


51    "Bell Anthem"
      Purcell.   Verse Anthem, "Rejoice in the World alway"
      (Zimmerman 49)

In the verse anthem "Rejoice in The World alway,"
nicknamed "Bell Anthem," Henry Purcell introduced a descending scale in imitation of the ringing of the bells which
called the faithful to worship on a Sunday morning.   According to Dupré, one of Purcell's biographers, the Sunday
memory of pealing bells is very grateful to an Englishman's
ears, because it brings back memories of earliest childhood.


52    "The Bells of Moscow"
      Rachmaninoff.    Prelude for Piano in C♯ minor, op. 3
      no. 2

This famous piano piece has, in one edition, been so
nicknamed through a questionable though understandable
flight of imagination on the part of some editor.   Perhaps
the reason is that the music tries to create the impression
of bells and their overtones.


53    "The Bells of Zlonice" [Zlonické Zvony]
      Dvořák.   Symphony No. 1 in C minor   (Burghauser 9)

The accepted numeration for Dvořák's symphonies does
not correspond with their order of composition, since the
first four were unpublished or posthumously published.
They were not included in the official numeration so that
the real number five has been called number one.   However, the symphony now known to be actually number one is
this C minor one, popularly known as "The Bells of Zlonice."
It was discovered in 1923 in the musical collection of Dr.
Rudolf Dvořák.   At the time Dvořák composed this work he
was living in Zlonice and the bells were probably those of
the church.


54    "The Bird" [Der Vogel]
      Haydn.   String Quartet [Russian Quartet], op. 33 no. 3,
      in C major   (Hob. III, 39)

The most charming work of this set of Russian Quartets is this No. 3. The grace notes in the main subject of the first movement, which all four instruments take up in the development, suggest the chirping of birds and partly explain the nickname. The real bird movement is, however, the trio of the Scherzando, an unusually lovely duet between the first and second violins.

55 "Black Key"
   Chopin. Etude for Piano, op. 10 no. 5, in Gb major
   (Brown 57)

The nickname is an obvious one because only once during the entire piece does the right hand touch a white key. Chopin himself authorized the name in a letter to Julian Fontana dated April 25, 1839.

56 "The Black Mass"
   Scriabin. Sonata, op. 68 no. 9

According to Faubion Bowers [Scriabin, v. II, p. 244], Podgaetsky, one of Scriabin's great friends, dubbed this sonata. Scriabin especially loved its second theme. In conversation he called it "dormant or dreaming saintliness" but in his usual confusion between sensual passion and supernal passion he marked it in the score as "nascent languor." However, the theme develops "evilly" as the notation reads "a sweetness gradually becoming more and more caressing and poisonous." Perhaps this is the reason for the subtitle "The Black Mass."

57 "Brandenburg Concertos"
   J. S. Bach. Six Concertos for Orchestra: no 1 F major; no. 2 F major; no. 3 G major; no. 4 G major; no. 5 D major; no. 6 Bb major (BWV 1046-51)

These concertos were written for and dedicated to the Margrave of Brandenburg, Christian Ludwig. Bach probably met him at the Meiningen Court and the Margrave, who in modern times would be described as a "concerto fan," invited Bach to write some orchestral works for him.
   The following is part of the dedication which Bach originally wrote in French: "As I had the honour of playing before Your Royal Highness a couple of years ago, and as I

observed that you took some pleasure in the small talent
that heaven has given me for music, and in taking leave of
Your Royal Highness You honoured me with a Command to
send you some pieces of my composition, I now according
to your gracious orders, take the liberty of presenting my
very humble respect to your Royal Highness, with the present Concertos, which I have written for several instruments, humbly praying You not to judge their imperfection
by the severity of the fine and delicate taste that everyone
knows you to have for music, but rather to consider be-
nignly the profound respect and the very humble obedience
to which they are meant to testify" [Schweitzer, J. S. Bach,
v. 1, p. 404].


58    "The Brasilian"
      Křenek.  Sinfoniette for String Orchestra

    The composer has written the following concerning his
work:  "I called my Sinfoniette 'The Brasilian' in order to
distinguish it from other works, because I wrote it when I
was in Brasil [January-March 1952].  It is something like
Mozart's 'Prague' or 'Linz' Symphonies'. "


59    "Brazilian Quartet No. 2"
      Villa Lobos.  String Quartet No. 6 in E major

    Heitor Villa Lobos wrote two string quartets which he
subtitled "Brazilian."  Although both owe a debt to the folk
music of Brazil it is the second one that is the most popular.  And in the Andante, which is a delicately atmospheric
tone painting, one can hear the subtle sounds of a Brazilian
jungle on a summer's night.


60    "Brukenthal"
      Haydn.  Symphony No. 27 in G major  (Hob. I, 27)

    In the World Encyclopedia of Recorded Music, the Sym-
phony No. 27 is subtitled "Brukenthal" by Francis Clough,
one of the editors.  He writes:  "The Brukenthal subtitle
for Symphony No. 27 goes back to the Prague recording of
this work; whether in fact we actually coined the description
as Brukenthal Symphony or whether it was so called on the
record publicity I cannot now say. "
    However this symphony seems to be better known as

"Hermannstadt Symphony. " It was found in the summer palace of Samuel Freiherr von Brukenthal nearby.


61   "Bucolic Sonata"
     Scarlatti.  Sonata for Piano  (L. 488, K. 8)


62   "The Bullfinch" [Il Gardellino]
     Vivaldi.  (A) Concerto for Flute and Strings, op. 10 no.
     3, in D major  (F. VI, 14); (B) Concerto for Flute,
     Oboe, Violin, Bassoon and Continuo in D major
     (F. XII, 9)

These concertos derive their nicknames from the fact that the flute tries to imitate the sound of the bullfinch. The descriptive label is of benefit chiefly in giving greater freedom to the soloist.  The flute begins its solo with short "calls" accompanied by the strings in unison.  After a free cadenza there are new embellishments for the instrument, each in turn trying to sound more like the bird.


63   "Burlesca"
     Scarlatti.  Sonata for Piano  (L. 338, K. 450)


64   "Butterfly"
     Chopin.  Etude for Piano, op. 25 no. 9, in G♭ major
     (Brown 78)

The nickname, as with most of the nicknames for Chopin's pieces, has no authority except the imaginative idea of some publisher.  In this particular case, whoever attached the descriptive title did it most appropriately.  The étude is light, fluttery, and when well performed, gives the impression of the whirr of a butterfly.


65   "La Caccia" [The Hunt]
     Scarlatti.  Sonata for Piano  (L. 104 & 465, K. 159 &
     96)


66   "La Caccia" [The Hunt]
     Vivaldi.  Concerto for Violin, Strings and Organ in B♭
     major  (F. I, 29)

67    "The Call of the Quail" [Der Wachtelschlag]
      Haydn.   No. 6 of a Set of Piano Pieces for Musical
      Clocks   (Hob. XIX, 8)

      Pater Primitivus Niemecz, Prince Esterházy's librari-
an, was an expert in making little mechanical organs for
musical clocks.   In these he used music composed by his
friend, Haydn.   When Ann, the daughter of the Austrian
court conductor, Florian Gassmann, was christened, Haydn
presented Frau Gassmann with one of these musical clocks.
The family Gassmann nicknamed the little piece it played
"Call of the Quail" because the character of the accompaniment reminded them of the sound of the bird.


68    "Camberwell Green"   (see "Spring Song")
      Mendelssohn.   Piece for Piano, op. 62 no. 6, in A
      major


69    "La Campanella" [The Belltower]
      Paganini (transcr. for piano by Liszt).   Rondo movt of
      Concerto, op. 7 no. 2, in B minor

      In the principal theme of the Rondo movement of Niccolò
Paganini's Concerto in B minor, the silver bell echoes the
violin note three times.   Because of this effect Paganini
named the movement, "Rondo à la Clochette."
      This is the same Rondo that Liszt included in his
"Grandes Etudes de Paganini," under the subtitle "La Campanella."   Liszt transposed the original key of the piece to
G♯ minor and in the first statement of the theme followed
Paganini's writing very closely.   However, in repeating the
theme again and again, he followed his own bent and the
piece became a brilliant virtuoso feat for the pianist.


70    "Candle Symphony"   (see "Farewell Symphony")
      Haydn.   Symphony No. 45 in F♯ minor   (Hob. I, 45)


71    "Cantata Mass"
      Haydn.   Missa St. Ceciliae in C major   (Hob. XXII, 5)

      The Saint Cecilia Mass is subtitled "Cantata Mass" be-
cause it is written so that each small section of the part of
the liturgy is given a whole movement.   It is the most

extensive of all the composer's masses, and was probably
written for performance by a Viennese musicians' guild in
1771.
    According to H. C. Robbins Landon, in his book
Symphonies of Joseph Haydn, there is an old legend quoted
by Pohl which describes the work as having been composed
by Haydn to restore his honor damaged by the hastily written 'Nicolaimesse. "


72  "Capriccio"
    W. F. Bach.   Fantasie for Piano in D minor


73  "Capriccio"
    Scarlatti.   Sonata for Piano   (L. 375, K. 20)


74  "Capriccio Diabolico"
    Castelnuovo-Tedesco.   Capriccio for Guitar.

    The composer says that Segovia, the great guitarist,
suggested that he write a piece for guitar in homage to Paganini, who was a great admirer of that instrument.   Bearing this in mind and also the fact that Paganini's violin
music was so fiendishly difficult, Castelnuovo-Tedesco decided to subtitle his piece "Capriccio Diabolico. "


75   "Carignane"
     Jacques Ibert.   Arabesque for Bassoon and Piano

    The composer explains the subtitle by saying that Carig-
nane is the name of a city where Burgundy wine is made,
and because of the euphony of the name and the association
of wine and gaiety he decided to subtitle the gay, charming
piece "Carignane. "


76   "Carnaval de Pesth"
     Liszt.   Hungarian Rhapsody for Piano No. 9 in E♭ ma-
     jor

    The Rhapsody No. 9 has probably been so nicknamed
because the noisy character of the music tries to depict a
carnival.   This piece has also been scored for orchestra.
In that arrangement it is transposed to D major and is
known as Hungarian Rhapsody No. 6.

77 "Cartwheel"
  Chopin.  Etude for Piano, op. 25 no. 3, in F major
  (Brown 99)

Herbert Weinstock, in his book Chopin, The Man and
His Music, says of this piece: "A study in accents is the
third F major Etude, once widely known as the 'Cartwheel'
for manifest reasons.  All that it requires for producing its
full inherent beauty is a minute adherence to the phrasing,
accents and agogic signs" [p. 213].


78 "La Casa del diavolo" (see "The House of the Devil")
  Luigi Boccherini.  Symphony, op. 12 no. 4, in D minor
  (Gérard 506)


79 "The Cat Waltz"
  Chopin.  Waltz for Piano, op. 34 no. 3, in F major
  (Brown 118)

The nickname recalls an incident in which the composer's cat jumped on the keyboard and, running up and down
the keys, suggested the grace note passage in the fourth
section of the piece to him.


80 "The Cat's Fugue"
  Scarlatti.  Fugue for Harpsichord  (L. 499, K. 30)

The composer's cat was supposed to have walked over
the keyboard, striking notes that Scarlatti used for the subject of the fugue.  Ralph Kirkpatrick, the harpsichordist,
says, "It might be remarked that only a light-footed and
accurate cat, possibly a kitten, could refrain from involun-
tary neighboring tones on the flats and sharps of the Fugue
subject."


81 "La Céleste"
  J. C. Bach.  Symphony in E♭, op. 9 no. 2  (Andante
  arr. for piano)


82 "Celestial Gate"
  Hovhaness.  Symphony No. 6, op. 173

83    "La Chasse" [The Hunt; Jagd-Sonate]
      Beethoven.    Sonata for Piano, op. 31 no. 3, in E♭ ma-
      jor

It is the brilliant, rhythmic, hunt-like theme which opens the Finale of this sonata that has suggested the nickname.   Actually the nickname is as inappropriate to the
rest of the sonata as "Moonlight" is to the Finale of the C♯
minor Sonata, op. 27 no. 2.

84    "La Chasse"
      J. L. Dussek.    Duo for Violin and Piano, op. 8, in C
      major

85    "La Chasse" (See 303, "The Hunt")
      Haydn.    Symphony No. 73 in D major    (Hob. I, 73)

86    "La Chasse"  [The Hunt]
      Haydn.    String Quartet, op. 1 no. 1, in B♭ major
      (Hob. III, 1)

It is because of the horn call character of the opening
phrase that this string quartet has been nicknamed "La
Chasse. "

87    "La Chasse" [The Hunt]
      Paganini.    Caprice for Violin No. 9 in E major

A caprice is a short instrumental piece, often in quick
tempo, which has surprises or whimsical effects of rhythm.
This one has the special effect of a hunting theme in double
stops which has given it its nickname.

88    "Chopsticks"
      Borodin, Cui, Liadov, Rimsky-Korsakov, & Liszt.
      Paraphrases for Four Hands at One Piano

The term "Chopsticks" is applied to a quick waltz tune
for four hands at the piano.   It is usually played by two
schoolgirls for amusement but is performed in a very traditional manner.   The hand is held flat in a perpendicular
position so that the notes are struck with the side of the

little finger. Added to this one finger melody played in the treble is a tonic dominant vamping bass part.

These Paraphrases for Four Hands are based on the "Chopsticks" theme. In an edition of the piece published in Leipzig in 1893, there is the following preface (originally in French): "Paraphrases. / 24 Variations and 15 small pieces for Piano on a favorite Theme.

Dedicated to small pianists capable of executing the theme with one finger of each hand. By Alexandre Borodin, César Cui, Anatole Liadov et Nicolas Rimsky-Korsakov. New Edition / Augmented with a Variation by Franz Liszt." [From the edition published by M. B. Belaieff, Leipzig, 1893.]


89    "Choral Prélude for Christmas"
      Barber.   Die Natali (for Orchestra)

This is an arrangement of Christmas carols for orchestra. The composer entitled the work "Die Natali" and subtitled it "Choral Prélude for Christmas." It had its first performance during the Christmas season of 1960 by the New York Philharmonic Orchestra.


90    "Choral Symphony"
      Beethoven.   Symphony No. 9, op. 125, in D minor

This is the English nickname for Beethoven's Ninth Symphony. It undoubtedly originated from the fact that the composer introduced words into a symphony for the first time. The baritone has a recitative which is immediately followed by a solo quartet and chorus set to the first three verses of Schiller's "Ode to Joy."

The following is an interesting anecdote about the dedication of the Symphony. In October 1826, Beethoven wrote to Frederick William III, King of Prussia, telling him that he was dedicating the Ninth Symphony to him. The King answered, saying that he was very pleased and that he would send Beethoven a diamond ring. When the ring arrived Beethoven discovered that the stone was not a diamond, but a cheap reddish one. This angered Beethoven tremendously and he sold the ring to the court jeweler; he threatened also to withdraw the dedication, but this he did not do.

CHRISTMAS                    22

91    "Christmas Concerto"
      Corelli.    Concerto Grosso, op. 6 no. 8, in G minor

    As the inscription, "Fatto per la Notte di Natale," indi-
cates, the work was composed for performance at Christmas
eve.   The fact is emphasized by the tender, hushed music
of the Pastoral, which suggests the mystery about to be revealed in the manger at Bethlehem.


92    "Christmas Concerto"
      Pietro Locatelli.    Concerto Grosso, op. 1 no. 8


93    "Christmas Concerto"
      Francesco Manfredini.    Concerto in C major   (from the
      1718 set)


94    "Christmas Concerto"
      Giuseppe Torelli.    Concerto Grosso, op. 8 no. 6


95    "Christmas Oratorio [Weihnachts-Oratorium]
      J. S. Bach.    Six Church Cantatas   (BWV 248)

    These six cantatas served for Christmas Day and the
two days following, the Feast of the Circumcision, the Sunday after the Circumcision, and the Feast of the Epiphany.
It is because of this that the subtitle originated.   The words
were written and compiled by Picander and Bach and the
music was composed in 1734.


96    "Christmas Sonata"
      Pietro Locatelli.    Sonata, op. 5 no. 5


97    "Christmas Symphony"
      Francesco Manfredini.    Symphony, op. 2 no. 12, in D
      major


98    "Classical Symphony"
      Prokofiev.    Symphony No. 1, op. 25, in D major

    It is said that in writing his Symphony No. 1, subtitled

"Classical Symphony," the composer chose the classical idiom partly to prove that he knew it and partly to tease his detractors, but mostly "from a desire to renovate, not to imitate, the classical form. " The ideas was to "write a symphony as Mozart might have written it had he been a contemporary. "


99   "The Clock" [Die Uhr]
     Haydn.   Symphony No. 101 in D major   (Hob. I, 101)

     In the Andante movement of the D major Symphony there is an accompanying figure played by the bassoons and plucked strings which gives the effect of the tick-tocking of a clock. It is because of this that the symphony has always been known as "The Clock. "


100  "The Cockcrow"
     Beethoven.   Sonata for Violin and Piano, op. 96, in G
     major

     Pierre Rode, the celebrated violinist, visited Vienna in 1812 and Beethoven wrote this Sonata in G major for him. It had its performance by him and the Archduke Rudolph on December 29, 1812, at the palace of Prince Lobkowitz.
     Rode's playing at the time was on the decline, and perhaps the fanciful nickname "Cockcrow" was given to it sarcastically.   Beethoven, in a letter to the Archduke, felt obliged to say that he had been "embarrassed by the necessity of avoiding 'rushing and resounding passages' which were not in Rode's style. "


101  "Coffee Cantata" [Kaffee-Cantate]
     J. S. Bach.   Cantata 211   (BWV 211)

     In the 18th century many princes forbade the public or private drinking of coffee in their dominions.   Picander wrote a text, published in 1727, concerning this very important issue and Bach composed the music for the well known "Coffee Cantata. "
     The theme of Picander's poem is as follows:   Father Schlendrian wishes to break his daughter, Lieschen, of the coffee habit, but she pleads with her father "If I do not drink my little cup of coffee three times a day, I shall be like a dried up piece of roast goat's flesh. " Finally in desperation

COLLECTIVE 24

she gives her ultimatum. "No wooer need come to the house unless he will promise and have it put into the marriage settlement that I may have the liberty to make coffee when I will."

In speaking of Bach's music for this text, Schweitzer says "It seems more to come from Offenbach than the old Cantor of St. Thomas" [J. S. Bach, v. II, p. 279].

102 "Collective Farm Symphony"
Nicolas Miaskovsky. Symphony No. 12, op. 35, in G minor

When the Symphony No. 12 was completed on December 12, 1931, the composer dedicated it to the 15th anniversary of the October Revolution. The reason for the subtitle is explained by the composer in the following: "When the first call to collectivization of peasant agriculture was sounded I was very much taken by this measure, which seemed most revolutionary in its consequence.... Almost instantly I conceived the musical image of a symphony about rural life in three stages, before, during the struggle for the new order, and finally after the completion of that struggle. In the Autumn of 1931 I began to work on my project" [quoted from Nicolas Slonimsky's Music Since 1900, p. 349].

103 "Compliments"
Beethoven. String Quartet, op. 18 no. 2, in G major

This quartet is identified in Germany by its nickname "Compliments Quartett." It is the most ingratiating of all of Opus 18 and particularly so because of the first four bars and replique which are supposed to convey the idea of "bowing and scraping." Cobbett thought the music might even suggest an elaborate reception at some rococo court like Schoenbrunn or Potsdam [Cyclopedic Survey, v. I, p. 107].

104 "Confidence" (see "Songs Without Words")
Mendelssohn. Piece for Piano, op. 19 no. 4, in A major

105 "The Consecration of the House" [Die Weihe des Hauses]
Beethoven. Overture, op. 124, in C major

Beethoven wrote this overture for the opening of the Josephstadt Theatre in Vienna, October 3, 1822. The newly organized orchestra did not receive the music until the afternoon before the opening of the theatre and Beethoven had requested that he conduct the performance from the piano. He could still hear a little but the performance would have been a disaster had not the Kapellmeister stood behind him, unseen, and helped direct the orchestra.


106   "The Consecration of Sound" [Die Weihe der Töne]
      Louis Spohr. Symphony No. 4, op. 86

In the autobiography of Spohr there is a letter written by him on October 9, 1832, telling of his newly completed Fourth Symphony which was inspired by Karl Pfeiffer's poem, "Die Weihe der Töne." He requested that the poem either be read out loud before the symphony was played or else that it be printed on the program.
       This symphony has also been subtitled "The Power of Sound," and "A Characteristic Tone Painting in the Form of a Symphony After a Poem by Karl Pfeiffer." Both in England and America the symphony is generally known by the subtitle "The Consecration of Sound."


107   "Consolation" (see "Songs Without Words")
      Mendelssohn. Piece for Piano, op. 30 no. 3, in E
      major


108   "Contemplation" (see "Songs Without Words")
      Mendelssohn. Piece for Piano, op. 30 no. 1, in E♭
      major


109   "Contredanse"
      Mozart. Serenade No. 2 in F major  (K. 101)

The second serenade, subtitled "Contredanse," was written for the carnival season at Salzburg. It is in four short movements which are light and gay in character.


110   "Corelli Fugue"
      J. S. Bach. Organ Fugue in B minor  (BWV 579)

Bach borrowed two subjects from Corelli's Opus 3, No. 4 and wrote the expressive double fugue which has been nick-named "Corelli Fugue. " The interesting thing is that Corelli said all he had to in 39 bars but Bach found material enough for over a hundred.

111  "La Cornara"
     Giovanni Legrenzi.    Sonata for Violin, op. 2, in D
     minor

This Sonata was written for the wife of a Venetian nobleman who was known as La Cornara.

112  "Il Corneto da Posta" [The post-horn]
     Vivaldi.    Concerto for Violin, Strings and Harpsichord
     in Bb major   (F. I, 163)

113  "Coronation Anthems"
     Handel.    Four Anthems for Voice and Orchestra

These anthems were written for the coronation of George II on October 11, 1727.   They were performed in Westminster Abbey with a large orchestra accompanying the vocal parts.   A new organ was especially built for the performance and a double bassoon was used for the first time in the orchestra.   The "bassoon-grosso" as it was called in Handel's scores, was designed and made by Stanesby, a flute maker under the supervision of Handel himself.
The Bishop of London was supposed to have selected and sent a list of texts to Handel for these anthems but Handel took offense at this and wrote to him saying "I have read my Bible well, and will choose for myself" [Williams, Handel, p. 94].

114  "Coronation Concerto" [Kronungs-Konzert]
     Mozart.    Concerto for Piano in D major (K. 537)

This concerto was given its nickname by André, not because of its particular regal quality, but because Mozart took it to Frankfurt in October 1790 and performed it during the coronation festivities of Leopold II.

115  "Coronation Mass" [Kronungs-Messe]
Mozart.   Mass in C major   (K. 317)

Mozart composed the "Coronation Mass" for annual service at the Church of Maria Plain, a shrine on the bank of
the Salzach, near Salzburg.   The Coronation of the Virgin
was commemorated by a service on the fifth Sunday after
Pentecost.

116  "Cortège"
Scarlatti.   Sonata for Piano   (L. 23, K. 380)

117  "The Cosmos"
Johan Franco.   Symphony No. 5

The composer writes the following about his symphony:
"The subtitle for my Fifth Symphony--which correctly should
be listed as "The Cosmos"--grew out of the book Journey
Into Strange Land; A Metaphysical Exploration of Ultimate
Truth, written by my wife, Eloise Franco and published in
1956 by Richard R. Smith.   The recording jacket unfortunate-
ly lists the title incorrectly on the front and the four move-
ments incorrectly on the back.   They should read: Symphony
V 'The Cosmos'  'The Beginning'  'Nocturne' (Region of the
Stars)  'Music of the Spheres' (The Planets 'Earth and
Man')   These follow the plan of the book in depicting the
coming forth of the universe.
"In the Beginning was the Light of the Holy Spirit.
What appears to us as the Manifest world was caused by the
descent of this Light through the Stars, the Planets, the
Earth and Man.   Final fulfillment will come through the up-
liftment of all again to Spirit. "

118  "The Cracow Mazurka"
Chopin.   Mazurka for Piano in A minor, op. 59bis
    (Brown 134)

This mazurka was published by Schott in an album entitled "Notre Temps" which was the general title of 12 piano
pieces composed by 12 different composers.   The English
publisher Wessel took the mazurka out of the Album and published it with this subtitle.

119  "Creation Mass" [Schöpfungmesse]
     Haydn.  Mass in B♭ major  (Hob. XXII, 13)

The "Creation Mass" of 1801 is so called because the
"Qui Tollis" quotes the melody of the Allegro section of
Adam and Eve's duet from Haydn's oratorio, The Creation.

120  "Credo Mass"
     Mozart.  Mass in C major  (K. 257)

The popular name "Credo" was given to this mass because of all the credos of Mozart the one in this mass is
perhaps the one in which he has tried the hardest to find a
fitting musical expression for the text.  The word "credo,"
wherever it occurs, is given to a simple staccato theme of
its own, always in unison, which remains distinct from the
general musical texture of the movement.

121  "The Crème de Menthe Variation"
     Rachmaninoff.  24th Variation of Rhapsody on a Theme
       of Paganini

According to the well-known pianist, Benno Moisewitsch,
Rachmaninoff and he met at a dinner party at the home of
Mrs. Steinway after one of Rachmaninoff's Carnegie Hall
concerts.  During dinner Rachmaninoff discussed his new
work, "Rhapsody on a Theme of Paganini," and how
fiendishly difficult the 24th variation with all the chord jumps
was to play.
       Later in the evening, when the butler came around
with a tray of wonderful liqueurs, Rachmaninoff, in his usual
manner of abstention, declined.  Moisewitsch remarked that
the best thing in the world for "jumps" was to drink a glass
of crème de menthe.  Rachmaninoff drank some, went to the
piano and played the variation perfectly.  Eyewitness ac-
counts and Rachmaninoff's own assertion have it that after
this incident he always drank a glass of crème de menthe
before playing the rhapsody in public.  Hence the superscription to the final variation, "The Crème de Menthe Variation. "

122  "Crown Imperial"
     William Walton.  Coronation March for Orchestra

The British Broadcasting Company commissioned Walton to write a work for the occasion of the coronation of George VI. He wrote this glittering Coronation March, subtitled "Crown Imperial" in which he paid homage to Elgar, whose works he greatly admired. It was first performed on May 9, 1937, and repeated in Westminster Abbey before the actual ceremony of the Coronation Day on May 22.

123 "The Cuckoo and the Nightingale"
    Handel.   Concerto No. 13 in F major for Organ

The nickname is derived from the passages which imitate the songs of birds. These were added when the organ adaptation was made by Walsh from the Concerto for Orchestra. (The second set of six were all arranged for organ.) This is one of the rare instances of imitative music in Handel's instrumental writings.

124 "The Cuckoo Concerto" [Il Cucù]
    Vivaldi.   Concerto for Violin in A major   (F. I, 223)

According to Pincherle, "The Cuckoo Concerto," of which no other edition than the English is known, was played so often that connoisseurs joked about it. This "Cuckoo Piece" somewhat annoyed the violinist Geminiani, because in his book, The Art of Playing The Violin (London 1751), he warned the reader that he will not find a way to imitate "The cock, cuckoo, owl and other birds--such tricks rather belong to the professors of legerdemain than to the art of music" [Vivaldi, Genius of the Baroque, p. 256].

125 "Cuckoo Sonata"
    Beethoven.   Sonata, op. 79, in G major

This has been nicknamed so because of the recurring three notes in the left hand of the first movement which fit the song of the cuckoo.

126 "Czech Suite" [Česká Suita]
    Dvořák.   Suite for Orchestra, op. 39, in D major
    (Burghauser 93)

As a whole this suite is a very characteristic and

national work and that is the reason that it has been so nicknamed.   The composition has five movements, each quite
different in mood.   The introductory movement is a Pastorale Prelude, the second a Melancholy Polka, the third a
Minuetto, the fourth a poetic Romanza and the fifth a fiery
Furiant.


127   "Danses des Nègres"
      Gottschalk.   Bamboula, op. 2, for Piano

      Jeanne Behrend has explained the subtitle (in her edi-
tion of some of Gottschalk's piano music): "Particularly
endearing to the Parisian public in later recitals were his
own [Louis Moreau Gottschalk's] compositions based on
Negro and Creole melodies from his native New Orleans.
'Who does not know the Bamboula?, raved a critic; Who is
there that has not read the description of that picturesque
dance that gives expression to the feeling of the negroes? '"


128   "Death and the Maiden" [Der Tod und das Mädchen]
      Schubert.   String Quartet, op. 161, in D minor  [D.
      810]

      The second movement of that string quartet in D minor
is based on the composer's song, "Death and the Maiden. "
As a matter of fact, the whole work seems to be inspired
with the poetic idea of the song, the picture of death as the
gentle friend of youth.   The quartet was written after a
period of illness and despair and thoughts of death were uppermost in Schubert's mind.


129   "Del Retiro"
      Vivaldi.   Concerto for Violin, Strings and Harpsichord
      in E♭ major  (F. I, 231)


130   "Deliciae Basilienses" [Baslerian delights]
      Honegger.   Symphony No. 4

      The reason for the subtitle of Symphony No. 4 is best
explained in the following notes of the composer:  "The first
movement dating from June, 1946, expresses precisely a
state of spirit.   In the midst of odious and stupid conditions
of life which are imposed upon us, it raises the hope of

escape from such an atmosphere.... The second movement
is based on the old popular song of Basel. The Finale is
of polyphonic construction in which the various components
are progressively superposed. From all of this there leaps
forth the tune 'Basler Morgenstreich.' Because of the
quotations of these characteristic songs, but even more for
personal reasons, I have employed the subtitle ''Deliciae
Basilienses'. ''

131    ''The Departure'' (see ''Songs Without Words'')
       Mendelssohn.   Piece for Piano, op. 62 no. 2, in B♭
       major

132    ''Dernière pensée musicale de Louis van Beethoven''
       (see ''Last Musical Thought'')
       Beethoven.   Piece for Piano in B♭ major   (WoO 60)

133    ''Desperation''
       Chopin.   Prelude, op. 28 no. 8, in F♯ minor   (Brown
       107)

The eminent conductor and pianist Hans von Bülow made
an analysis of the 24 preludes of Chopin's Op. 28, which
was recorded by his pupil, Laura Rappoldi-Kahrer. Each
was given a title and a description in the characteristic
manner of German Romanticism. Of No. 8 he says: ''We
owe this prélude to a real occurrence which Liszt mentions
in his life of Chopin. One day George Sand had gone out
on an excursion with her son Maurice; they were surprised
by a heavy storm and did not return until the next day,
when Chopin, terrified by their unexplained absence, played
it in such a state of nervous excitement that he seemed
bereft of his senses. With a face as pale as ashes he gazed
fixedly at her, apparently without knowing who she was.
The small notes, which wind throughout almost all the keys
by means of chromatic and enharmonic modulations, picture
his feverish anxiety and ever increasing frenzy; the thumb
of the right hand intones an exquisite melody, distinguished
by beauty as well as by passion. Shortly before the close
he seems to recognize the features of his loved one (F
sharp major, sixth measure from the end); but almost immediately they fade (F sharp minor, third measure from the
end), and again desperation reigns'' [Musician, xvi (1911)].

134   "Der deutsche Michel" (see "The German Michel")
      Bruckner.  Symphony No. 8 in C minor


135   "The Devil's Chuckle" (see "Le Rire du Diable")
      Paganini.  Caprice for Violin, No. 13, in B♭ major


136   "Devil's Trill" [Il Trillo del Diavolo]
      Giuseppe Tartini.  Sonata for Violin in G minor

      One night in the year 1713, Tartini relates, in a dream
he made a compact with the devil, who promised to be at
his service on all occasions.  Ultimately, the two became
so familiar that Tartini presented his Satanic Majesty with
his violin to find out what sort of musician he was.  Tartini was
astounded to hear the devil play so beautifully, with such
taste and skill that he says he never had heard music performed so exquisitely in his whole life.
      In a state of feverish excitement, Tartini awoke and
instantly seized his fiddle in hopes of repeating what he had
just heard, but alas, the devil had gone and his music with
him.  Nevertheless, he was inspired and the result is the
"Devil's Trill. "


137   "Di Tre Re"
      Honegger.  Symphony No. 5

      This nickname means "Of Three D's, " the word "re"
being the second note in the syllables of the scale.  Each of
the three movements ends with a pizzicato and a stroke of
the tympani on D.   John N. Burk suggests that "The fanciful
sobriquet merely affirms the suitability of three quiet end-
ings, for a symphony so dark in color and so sober, however profound or personal in feelings. "


138   "Diabelli Variations"
      Beethoven.   33 Variations on a Theme of Diabelli for
      Piano in C major, op. 120

      The Viennese publisher, Diabelli, wrote a very unim-
portant waltz and invited Schubert, Beethoven and other composers to write variations on it.  At first Beethoven declined, saying that he did not want to write variations on a
"Schusterfleck" ("cobbler's patch") but he reconsidered it and

wrote 33 variations on the theme.

Hans von Bülow, in his edition of the piano music of Beethoven, has called the work the "Mikrokosmos of Beethoven's genius. " John N. Burk, in The Life and Works of Beethoven, says, "Here is an outstanding instance where a theme of no consequence, but of eminent serviceability, became so firmly implanted in Beethoven's mind that he could not let go of it until he took it through as many forms and paces that he could possibly think of" [p. 456].

139  "Didone Abbandonata"
     Clementi.   Sonata for Piano, op. 50 no. 3, in G minor

The nickname is used in the first edition of Muzio Clementi's Sonatas published in London in 1821, the only other notation being the words "Scena Tragica. "

140  "Didone Abbandonata"
     Giuseppe Tartini.   Sonata for Violin and Piano in G
     minor

There is, as far as we know, no specific account of what prompted Tartini to compose a Sonata built around the theme of Dido deserted by Aeneas at Carthage.   The lament of the opening Adagio is unmistakable.

The second movement may or may not create a vision of the raging flames of Dido's self-appointed funeral pyre, but in any case the following pacing march could only be a procession of mourners.   The dancing finale, still in the minor, is appropriate in suggesting a kind of Elysian release for the grieving Dido after death.

141  "Dissonant"
     Mozart.   String Quartet in C major   (K. 465)

Mozart wrote a set of six string quarters which he dedicated to his "very celebrated and most dear friend, " Joseph Haydn.   The last of the set, the one in C major, has been nicknamed "Dissonant" because of the introductory Adagio.   In our time these 21 bars seem musically logical, but in Mozart's day they raised no end of discussion. Haydn's comment was, "Since Mozart wrote it this way, he must have had good reason to do so. "

142   "Il Distratto" [The Distraught]
      Haydn.  Symphony No. 60 in C major  (Hob. I, 60)

      The Symphony No. 60 was written in 1775 and one of
the reasons for its name was that it was written originally
as a sort of suite based on Haydn's incidental music to the
comedy Il Distratto.  Another reason is that there are several amusing and "distraught" bits of writing in the work.
      In the first movement, after a long diminuendo,
there is a sudden loud tutti featuring the tympani, then an
unexpected fanfare is heard in the Adagio, but the biggest
surprise of all, and one that was certain to amuse any audience of the 18th century, is in the Finale.  After a grand
pause of the whole orchestra Haydn required the violinists
to retune their instruments.  The E, A and D string were
correct but when the men tried the G string they discovered
that the pitch had gone down to F.  Not paying any attention
to the listening audience, the players raised the lowest
string again to G and continued on as though nothing had
happened.  To play wrong notes purposely in order to pro-
duce a humorous result was one of the oldest and most effective devices.


143   "La Divina"
      Luigi Boccherini.  Symphony No. 15 in D minor
      (Gérard 517)

      The only accountable reason for this nickname is that
the symphony is more serious and reflective than most of
Boccherini's work.  The title was first used in a faulty edition by Sondheimer (Basel, 1934).  He used only the first
two movements and the third and fourth movements were
from Symphony Op. 35, No. 1.


144   "The Dog Waltz"  (see "Minute Waltz")
      Chopin.  Waltz for Piano, op. 64 no. 1, in Db major
      (Brown 164, no. 1)


145   "Dominicus"  (see "Pater Dominicus")
      Mozart.  Mass in C major  (K. 66)


146   "The Donkey"  (see "The Quinten")
      Haydn.  String Quartet, op. 76 no. 2, in D minor
      (Hob. III, 76)

147   "Das Donnerwetter"  (see "The Thunderstorm")
      Mozart.   Contretanz for Orchestra (K. 534)


148   "Dorian"
      J. S. Bach.    Toccata and Fugue for Organ in D minor
      (BWV 538)

      The Organ Toccata and Fugue in D minor was given
the nickname "Dorian" because its musical structure was
supposed to follow the pattern of the Dorian Mode.   (The
name Dorian is applied by Greek theorists as the species
of the octave ranging from D to D.)
      According to Grove's Dictionary of Music and Mu-
sicians, the piece is not in the Dorian Mode but in pure D
minor and the nickname is due to the fact that it is written
without a key signature.   At first sight this certainly suggests the Dorian Mode but the accidentals proper to D minor are casually inserted from bar to bar throughout the
piece.   In the Bach Gesellschaft edition of the organ works
this Toccata and Fugue is listed as "Dorian."


149   "Double Symphony"
      Louis Spohr.   Symphony No. 7, op. 121, in C major

      The symphony published by Schuberth of Hamburg
merely as opus 121 is better known by its nickname "Double
Symphony."   The title given to this work by Spohr was
"Irdisches und Göttliches im Menschenleben" ("worldly and
Godly in men's lives").   The origin of the symphony is attributed to a conversation Spohr had with his wife as to
what kind of a composition he might write that would really
be in a grand style.   She suggested, partly in jest, that if
a simple symphony were not enough, why shouldn't he write
a double symphony for two orchestras.
      Spohr accepted the suggestion and decided to repre-
sent the two principles of good and evil by using two orchestras.   The first subject was called "Kinderwelt" ("the world
of childhood"), the second, "Zeit der Leidenschaften" ("the
age of passions"), and the third, "Endlicher Sieg des Gött-
lichen" ("the final victory of the divine principle").   The
large orchestra represented the principle of evil and the
small one, consisting of only 11 solo instruments, the principle of good.

150 "The Dragon Fly"
 Chopin.  Prelude, op. 28 no. 11, in B major  (Brown
 107, no. 11)

Each of the Op. 28 preludes of Chopin was given a
subtitle by Hans von Bülow.  Of this one he writes, "It
flies in a circle round a pool; now it darts to the centre,
now to and fro--a last time--it sinks in the water" [Musi-
cian, xvi (1911)].


151 "Dramatique"
 Anton Rubinstein.  Symphony No. 4, op. 95, in D
 minor

In this symphony the various instruments of the orchestra are introduced separately like characters in an
opera.  The music is full of monologues and dialogues
which give the symphony a dramatic feeling.  Rubinstein
went on a long tour of Germany in the beginning of 1870
and the symphony, by then popularly known as the "Dramatique," was most enthusiastically received.


152 "A Dream"
 Ned Rorem.  Lions--Poème for Orchestra

The composer explains his subtitle in the following
manner:  "Twenty years ago, one morning after a dream I
wrote a poem called Lions.  The poem is lost but the
dream remains clearly still.  It opens into a room of ado-
lescence where I discovered music.  The sound of my time
before of the past.  (In such a room ignorant of Bach,
Chopin even Tchaikovsky I used to hear recorded screams
of Varèse and Milhaud, tango of Ravel and Stravinsky)....
Today I reconstruct the forgotten poem in orchestration."


153 "Dream Quartet"
 Haydn.  String Quartet, op. 50 no. 5, in F major
 (Hob. III, 48)

The slow movement of the quartet, Op. 50, No. 5,
which has some elaborate solo passages for the violin, is
known as "A Dream."  It is because of this movement that
the quartet was given its nickname.

154    "Drum Roll"
       Haydn.  Symphony No. 103 in E♭ major  (Hob. I, 103)

       The symphony starts with a long unaccompanied roll of
the kettle drums.  It is because of this romantic and highly
dramatic introduction that the nickname originated.


155    "The Drumstroke" [Der Paukenschlag]  (see "Surprise
       Symphony")
       Haydn.  Symphony No. 94 in G major  (Hob. I, 94)


156    "Der Dudelsack"  (see "The Bagpipes")
       Haydn.  (Russian) Dance No. 16  (Hob. XIX, 4)


157    "The Duel"
       Chopin.  Prelude, op. 28 no. 12, in G♯ minor
       (Brown 107, no. 12)

       Hans von Bülow, in giving this prelude a subtitle (as
he did all the Op. 28 preludes), commented, "As is well
known, Chopin was of a jealous disposition--and so far as
George Sand was concerned had every reason to be.  This
prélude represents a scene in which two rivals confront each
other armed with flashing swords.  The groups of two
eighth notes in the right hand may be compared to the con-
testants approaching each other (crescendo), then falling
back and again drawing near; while the left hand represents
three steps in each measure.  At the fortissimo shields are
heard to clash; at the piano the combatants retreat, only to
hurl themselves against each other (skips in the left hand).
This goes on until the swords flash (short chord in the left
hand); Chopin is wounded--assistance is brought (figure in
eighth notes, right hand)--great confusion--the injured one
is borne away" [Musician, xvi (1911)].


158    "Duet" [so named by composer]  (see "Songs Without
       Words")
       Mendelssohn.  Piece for Piano, op. 38 no. 6, in A♭
       major


159    "Dumky Trio"
       Dvořák.  Trio, op. 90, in E minor  (Burghauser 166)

This trio is unique because it is virtually the first
time in Dvořák's chamber music that the composer departed
from the conventional four-movement form and wrote a collection of six "dumky"--hence the nickname.  A dumka is
an elegy which may be expected to be melancholy in mood.
It also contains a middle section usually in fast tempo and
always contrasting sharply in mood with the elegiacal sections.

160   "Eagles"
      Ned Rorem.  Orchestral Study

    The composer has written the following concerning this
work:  "The inspiration for the subtitle 'Eagles' came from
Walt Whitman's poem 'The Dalliance of The Eagles.' ... I
am obsessed with literature.  Of all the arts extraneous to
my own, literature is the only one of importance to me.  I
am sympathetic to the 'poignance' of certain authors and have
their quality constantly in mind while writing music.  I must
say with a subtitle what the abstract sound will never di-
vulge. ... "

161   "Echo"
      Vivaldi.   Concerto for String Orchestra in A major
        (F. I, 139)

    The six "echo" concertos of Vivaldi are obviously oc-
casional works designed for the amusement of a frivolous
audience at some summer residence.  This particular one
in A major was discovered by Bernardino Molinari in the
Sächsische Landesbibliothek, Dresden, among a mass of
Vivaldi manuscripts.
    Vivaldi wrote this for string orchestra and an ac-
companying cembalo.  Against this he used a group of solo
instruments which echo the music of the tutti.  It is because of this device that the nickname was attached to the
concerto.

162   "Echo"
      Haydn.   Divertimento for Double String Trio in E♭
        major  (Hob. II, 39)

    Haydn loved to compose musical jokes for groups of
amateurs.  This divertimento is one of these "fun-loving"

compositions. It was composed for two groups of three players in each group who were seated in such a way that even though they were in different rooms they could see each other. Each group played music that echoed that of the other group.


163   "Edward"
       Brahms.   Ballade for Piano, op. 10 no. 1, in D minor

    This is the first of a set of four ballades and the inspiration for its subtitle was derived from the Scottish ballad "Edward. " This familiar and grisly ballad tells the gloomy story of the son who curses his mother for having goaded him into killing his father and abandoning his castle and wife and children.
    The three pages of the piece correspond to three acts of a play. In the first and third pages, the feeling of country, time and place is portrayed. In the middle page the hammering triplets depict a great feeling of passionate terror.


164   "Egyptian"
       Saint-Saëns.   Concerto for Piano No. 5, op. 103, in
       F major

    The second movement of the concerto, the Andante, was strongly influenced by Saint-Saëns' impression of his visit to Luxor on the Nile. It is because of this that the concerto has been nicknamed "Egyptian. "


165   "Elegiac Symphony"
       Pietro Locatelli.   Sinfonia in F minor


166   "Elegiaca"
       Giàn Francesco Malipiero.   Symphony No. 2

    Malipiero has stated, "In regard to my Second Symphony I want to avoid confusion and misunderstanding. I wish to refer at once to the subtitle 'Elegiaca. ' This qualificative is an explanation how music that I wrote in the anxious and tragic month of the year 1936, a year full of sadness, yet remains outside of the events and has elegiac

character.  This Symphony is just music. ...   I wish to emphasize that in the term elegiaca there is no intention of
program music" ["Composer's Notes," Seattle Symphony Orchestra program, January 25, 1937].

167   "Elégie harmonique sur la mort du Prince Louis
        Ferdinand"
      J. L. Dussek.   Sonata for Piano, op. 61, in F♯ minor

In 1803 at Magdeburg, Dussek became acquainted with
Prince Louis Ferdinand of Prussia.   This was the beginning
of a great friendship, and Dussek gave the Prince much advice on piano playing and composition.   It was because of
Prince Ferdinand's premature death on the field of Saalfeld
that in 1806 wrote this sonata in his memory.

168   "Elegy"
      Arnold Bax.   Trio for Flute, Viola and Harp in G ma-
        jor

169   "Elegy"  (see "Songs Without Words")
      Mendelssohn.   Piece for Piano, op. 85 no. 4, in E
        major

170   "Eleonoren Sonate"
      Beethoven.   Sonata for Piano in C minor   (WoO 51)

This is an easy piano sonata which Beethoven dedicated
to his young friend Eleonore von Breuning and it has always
been called "Eleonoren Sonate. "

171   "Emperor Concerto"
      Beethoven.   Concerto for Piano No. 5, op. 73, in E♭
        major

The year 1809, that of Beethoven's fifth and last piano
concerto, saw the invasion of Vienna by the armies of Napoleon.   The event caused Beethoven not only fierce anger but
grave discomfort.   He was forced to seek shelter in a cellar
and cover his ears so as not to hear the noise of the guns.
Later he is known to have said, "There was a disturbing
wild life around me with nothing but drums, cannons, men

and misery of all sorts. "
  His earlier admiration for Napoleon had entirely
disappeared and it is ironic that someone unknown, possibly
the pianist and publisher, J. B. Cramer, should have la-
belled the work with the nickname "Emperor Concerto. "
Beethoven would have undoubtedly protested against this.
The concerto was actually published in 1811 with a dedication to the Archduke Rudolph.


172  "The Emperor" [also "The Emperor's Hymn"]
     Haydn.  String Quartet, op. 76 no. 3, in C major
     [Hob. III, 77]

  "The Emperor" has the famous variations on Haydn's
own hymn, "Gott erhalte Franz den Kaiser. "  There are
four variations and in each a different member of the quartet
is given the melody.  This hymn was a great favorite of
Haydn's and it is known that on May 26, 1809, five days
before he died, Haydn called in his servants for the last
time and had them carry him to the piano where he solemnly played the "Emperor's Hymn" three times in succession.


173  "English Suites"
     J. S. Bach.  Six Suites for Piano:  no. 1 A major;
        no. 2 A minor; no. 3 G minor; no. 4 F major;
        no. 5 E minor; no. 6 D minor  (BWV 806-811)

  It is said that in a manuscript copy of these suites the
first one had the inscription, "fait pour les Anglais. "  Forkel, Bach's first biographer, also felt that they were written for an Englishman and probably one of high standing.


174  "The English Symphony"
     Dvořák.  Symphony No. 4 [new no. 8] in G major, op.
        88  (Burghauser 163)

  It seems that Dvořák was annoyed with his publisher
Simrock when the matter of this symphony was discussed.
Simrock offered Dvořák 1000 marks for it on condition that
he would receive some smaller works in the bargain.  This
was too insulting to Dvořák and he took his score to London
where he offered it to Novello and Company.  It was accepted immediately; this supposedly was the origin of the
nickname.

Actually, it is not too fitting a nickname because the work is very Bohemian in character and Dvořák had originally intended it as a token of his appreciation for being elected to the "Bohemian Academy of Emperor Franz Joseph for the Encouragement of Art and Literature."

175 "Enigma Variations"
Elgar. Variations for Orchestra on an Original Theme, op. 36

The idea of composing such a set of variations came to Edward Elgar one day when he was extemporizing at the piano. When they were complete, he wrote as a dedication "To my friends pictured within" and explained to one of them, "I have labeled 'em with the nickname of my particular friends--that is to say, I have tried to imagine the party writing the variation him (or her) self, and have written what I think they would have written--if they were asses enough to compose." Each variation is headed by the letters of a friend's name or nickname by which he was known.

176 "Erdödy Quartets"
Haydn. String Quartets, op. 76 (Hob. III, 75-80)

In the years 1797-8 six string quartets were published as Op. 76 with a dedication to Count Erdödy.

177 "Eroica"
Beethoven. Sonata for Violin and Piano, op. 30 no. 2, in C minor

This sonata is sometimes referred to as the "Eroica" because it reveals with remarkable completeness the Beethoven in whom thoughts of the "Eroica" Symphony were first stirring. It is music of great tranquillity.

178 "Eroica"
Beethoven. Symphony No. 3 in E♭ major, op. 55

In the beginning of the 1800's Beethoven watched the startling rise of Napoleon with deep interest. To him the great Corsican appeared as the champion of an ideal free-

dom, and it was in his honor that the "Eroica" was composed and named. Early in the spring of 1804 the score
was ready to go to Paris with Napoleon's name on the title
page when the news arrived that Napoleon had proclaimed
himself Emperor. In a fit of rage and disappointment that
his hero should prove so false to the conception that he had
of him Beethoven tore out the dedication and substituted that
of his Serene Highness Prince Lobkowitz.

179  "Eroica"
      MacDowell.   Sonata for Piano, op. 50, in G minor

The "Eroica" bears the motto, "Flos regum Arthuris. "
As a further explanation of the music MacDowell says that
he did not write the sonata exactly as program music, even
though he had the Arthurian legend in mind when he
composed the work. He used the name "Eroica" rather as
a subtitle.
      The composer explains the music still further by
saying that the first movement typifies the coming of Arthur,
the second was suggested by a picture by Gustave Doré
showing a knight in the woods surrounded by elves, and the
third movement, by MacDowell's idea of Guinevere.


180   "Eroica Variations"
      Beethoven.   Fifteen Variations and Fugue for Piano,
         op. 35, in E♭ major

The 15 variations and fugue, Op. 35, are based on a
theme from Beethoven's ballet, Die Geschöpfe des Prometheus ("The creatures of Prometheus" or "the men of Prometheus"). The same theme appears later in the finale of the
Eroica Symphony. Despite the fact that the variations were
written before the symphony, they have always been referred
to as the "Eroica Variations. "


181   "Espansiva"
      Carl Nielsen.   Symphony No. 3, op. 27

The subtitle is not meant to be taken programatically.
It simply refers to the growth of the mind and spirit and
the widening of life's horizons.

182  "Etats d'Ame" [Soul States]
     Scriabin.   Sonata No. 3, op. 23, in F♯ minor

     This sonata was written at a critical time in Alexander
Scriabin's life.   His marriage was about to fall apart and
his artistic vision was changing rapidly.   Scriabin subtitled
this sonata "Etats d'Ame" because he felt that this music
was an emotional biography.
     Faubion Bowers in his book, Scriabin [v. 1, p. 254],
says the following: "Musically the Sonata reverberates with
proud, ponderous noble emphasis of heavy chords.   It
spreads widely over the keyboard with large intervals of
space, windows for the sound to be heard through.   Mixed
into this voyage of soul are whiplashes of tempestuous winds
and waves out of which bursts the Man-God.   An emotional
biography, it saves his Soul. "


183  "Etudes in Form of Variations"
     Schumann.   Etudes Symphoniques for Piano, op. 13,
     in C♯ minor

     Schumann hesitated a long time about the choice of the
title, "Etudes Symphoniques. "   He considered in turn
"Davidsbündlerétuden" and "Etudes in Orchestral Character. "
He finally adopted the name "Etudes Symphoniques" and the
understandable subtitle "Etudes in Form of Variations. "
     An amateur, Hauptman von Fricken, had sent a
composition of his own, a theme with variations for flute,
to Wieck and Schumann for criticism.   Schumann was attracted to the theme, took it, improved upon it with various
changes, and wrote his well known "Etudes Symphoniques. "


184  "The Evening Star" (see "Songs Without Words")
     Mendelssohn.   Piece for Piano, op. 38 no. 1, in E♭
     major


185  "F. A. E. (Frei aber einsam)" [free but lonely]
     A. H. Dietrich, Brahms, Schumann.   Sonata for Violin
     and Piano

     Albert Herman Dietrich, a pupil of Robert Schumann
and friend of Johannes Brahms, collaborated with Schumann
and Brahms in composing this sonata as a greeting to Joachim on his arrival at Düsseldorf in 1853.   It was intended

to be a humorous work and that is the reason for the subtitle.

Dietrich wrote the opening movement (A minor); Schumann, the Intermezzo (F major) and the finale (F minor); and Brahms, the third movement, a Scherzo (C minor). When Joachim played through the sonata for the first time with Clara Schumann he recognized the respective composers immediately.


186   "Faith"   (see "Songs Without Words")
      Mendelssohn.   Piece for Piano, op. 102 no. 6, in C
      major


187   "The Fall of Warsaw"   (see "Revolutionary")
      Chopin.   Etude for Piano, op. 10 no. 12, in C minor
      (Brown 67)


188   "[24] Fantasy Pieces after the Zodiac for amplified
      Piano"
      George Crumb.   Makrokomos, Vol. I. and II.

The composer wrote about the subtitle, "Each volume has a piece written on each of the 12 Zodiac signs. Thus, in the two volumes I run through the Zodiacal set twice." Volume one was written in 1972 and Volume two in 1973.


189   "The Farewell"
      J. L. Dussek.   Sonata for Piano in E♭ major, op. 44


190   "A Farewell"   (see "Songs Without Words")
      Mendelssohn.   Piece for Piano, op. 85 no. 2, in A
      minor


191   "Farewell Symphony" (or, sometimes, "Candle Sym-
      phony")
      Haydn.   Symphony No. 45 in F minor   (Hob. I, 45)

There are two stories concerning this symphony: (1) It seems that Prince Esterhazy was so attracted to vacationing in Esterháza each year that the stays there became longer and longer. The musicians he brought with him, except

Haydn, were not permitted to have their families with them and they became very restless. Finally, at the end of the season of 1722, the men, in complete desperation, went to their beloved Haydn for help. The result was the "Farewell Symphony" in which Haydn, to make his point clear, changed the form of the Presto Finale. During this movement a long Adagio began in which one player after the other blew out the candle and departed. Only two players remained, Tomasini, the Prince's favorite violinist and Joseph Haydn himself. The Prince finally grasped the idea and was supposed to have said, "Well, if they all leave we might as well leave too." The next day the whole court departed.

(2) In the newly revised Baker's Biographical Dictionary of Musicians (5th ed. , 1958-71), by Nicolas Slonimsky, there is an interesting account [on p. 677] of the nicknaming of the "Farewell Symphony." Slonimsky says that instead of the commonly accepted story (above), he has found a more plausible explanation in a little known book by an Italian friend of Haydn, Giacomo Gotifredo Ferrari, published in London in 1830. According to Ferrari's version, the Prince intended to disband the orchestra and Haydn's "Farewell Symphony" was a stratagem to move the patron's heart and to save the orchestra. Obviously it succeeded.

192 "Fate Symphony" (also, "Victory Symphony")
    Beethoven. Symphony No. 5, op. 67, in C minor

Beethoven was supposed to have remarked to Schindler, regarding the opening motif of the Fifth, "Thus Fate knocks at the door." This may have reflected a momentary poetic mood but he also might have used the expression to try to stimulate the imagination of the rather inadequate orchestral players of the day to give more stirring interpretation to the works that they played.

During the Second World War the symphony acquired (among the Allies) the popular name of "Victory Symphony": the V is a symbol for Victory and "V" in Morse Code is dot, dot, dot, dash, or · · · —. This is the same rhythm as the main theme of the first movement.

193 "Les Favorites"
    Chopin. Polonaises for Piano, op. 26 and 40 (Brown
        90)

194   "Il Favorito"
      Vivaldi.   Concerto for Violin, Strings and Organ in E
      minor   (F. I, 208)


195   "Fear"
      Chopin.   Prelude, op. 28 no. 14, in E♭ minor   (Brown
      107, no. 14)

Each of the Op. 28 preludes of Chopin was given a
subtitle by Hans van Bülow.   He writes, "At the period of
his life when he was subjected to many nervous shocks Chopin suffered more than ever from hallucinations.   When he
sat at the piano in the twilight a throng of spectres sometimes seemed to pursue him, and his anguish became un-
speakable.   His whole being appeared to be agitated by in-
visible and violent impulses and he believed that he heard
the sound of similar concussions in the air around him.
One cannot rid himself of the feeling of fear in listening to
this short piece" [Musician, xvi (1911)].


196   "The Festino"
      Haydn.   Overture in D major (actually the 1st movt. of
      Symphony No. 53 in D major)   (Hob. I, 53)

According to Rosemary Hughes, in her book Haydn, the
first movement of the Symphony No. 53 in D became enor-
mously popular in England under this nickname.


197   "Feuersymphonie" [Fire Symphony]
      Haydn.   Symphony No. 59 in A major   (Hob. I, 59)

It is very possible that the Symphony No. 59 may have
actually been the overture to Haydn's opera, Die Feuerbrunst.   (The three-movement Overture to Acide is entitled
Sinfonia.)   The opera, which is really a German "Singspiel,"
had been thought to be spurious, but just recently, through
the efforts of the great Haydn scholar, H. C. Robbins Landon, the watermarks of the Singspiel manuscript were
checked and comparisons were made with well known Haydn
manuscripts in the Esterházy archives, and it had been
found to be authentic.
      The copy of the manuscript now at Yale University
was prepared during Haydn's lifetime from the original which
is now lost.   The copy was prepared by Johann Traeg, a

Viennese publisher, who owned at least half a dozen original
Haydn manuscripts by the end of the 18th century.   A dif-
ference exists between the name Haydn gave the opera, Das
abgebrannte Haus ("the house that burned down"), and that
given to it by the Traeg Catalogue, in which it is called
Die Feuerbrunst ("the fire") [from The New York Times,
June 4, 1961].

198   "Fiddle Fugue"
      J. S. Bach.   Fugue for Organ in D minor   (BWV 539)

     This fugue appeared first as a movement in G minor
in the first of the well-known six sonatas for violin solo.
After Bach transcribed it for the organ it became known as
the "Fiddle Fugue." Friedrich Griepenkerl, writing more
than 100 years ago, erred in supposing that the organ fugue
had been transcribed for violin.  Bach made a third version
of the piece, transcribing it for the lute (BWV 1000).

199   "De Fire Temperamenter"   (see "The Four Tempera-
         ments")
      Carl Nielsen.   Symphony No. 2 in B minor

200   "The Fist"
      Haydn.   Symphony No. 39 in G minor   (Hob. I, 39)

     According to C. G. Burke in his book, The Collector's
Haydn, this symphony is "sullen, vindictive and ominous, the
G minor tirade cuts its indelible way into memory while it
achieves an utmost felicity of art, growing as it lengthens,
and nearly two hundred years ago its effect was as it is today, for the young Mozart used it as a model for his own
early G minor Symphony No. 25, which musicologists have
lauded as a trailblazer while ignoring who did the blazing
first" [p. 171].   It seems that the "sullenness" and "omi-
nousness" have given rise to the fanciful but understandable
nickname.

201   "The Fleecy Cloud"   (see "Songs Without Words")
      Mendelssohn.   Piece for Piano in E♭ major, op. 53
         no. 2

202   "The Flight"   (see "Songs Without Words")
      Mendelssohn.   Piece for Piano, op. 53 no. 6, in A
      major


203   "Folk Song"
      Roy Harris.   Symphony No. 4 for Chorus and Orches-
      tra

This symphony is divided into seven movements and the
composer has used folk song material in at least five of
them.
      The well known "When Johnny Comes Marching
Home" is heard in the Finale, delightful cowboy songs are
interpolated into the second movement and the popular ditties
"Jump Up, My Lady" and "The Blackbird and the Crow" are
skillfully used in the fifth.


204   "La Follia"
      Vivaldi.   Sonata in D minor for two Violins and Cello
      (or harpsichord)   (F. XIII, 28)


205   "Die Forelle"   (see "The Trout")
      Schubert. Piano Quintet, op. 114, in A major   (D.
      667)


206   "The Four Seasons"
      Henry Hadley.   Symphony No. 2 in F minor, op. 30

The subtitle is explanatory of the four movements of
the symphony: "Winter" depicts the austerity and desolation
of that time of year; "Spring" is a cleverly orchestrated
Scherzo in which elves "dance and romp in the moonlight";
"Summer" is in a romantic mood with its main theme an
authentic Indian Love Song; and "Autumn" has a pretty theme
in staccato figures played by the violin and suggesting falling
leaves [from the Boston Post Herald, April 16, 1905].


207   "The Four Temperaments" [Die vier Temperamente]
      Hindemith.   Theme and Four Variations for Piano and
      String

In the 16th and 17th centuries there was the idea that

the various types of moisture in the human body, phlegm,
blood, choler and melancholy, were responsible for the
physical condition and mental outlook of the individual.    It
may be that Hindemith was influenced by this when he labeled
his variations, I. Melancholic, II. Sanguine, III. Phlegmatic,
and IV. Choleric.    This in turn influenced his subtitling of
the composition.

208   "The Four Temperaments" [De fire temperamenter]
      Carl Nielsen.    Symphony No. 2 in B minor

      The composer's tempo indications for the four move-
ments are:  Allegro collerico; Allegro commodo e flemma-
tico; Andante malincolo; Allegro sanguineo.    These refer to
the four bodily humours or temperaments and are the reason for the subtitle.

209   "French Suites"
      J. S. Bach.    Six Suites for Piano:  no. 1 D minor;
      no. 2 C minor; no. 3 B minor; no. 4 E♭ major;
      no. 5 G major; no. 6 E major  (BWV 812-817)

      It is not known how the "French Suites" received their
nickname and even the great Bach authority, Forkel, has no
precise information on that point.    However, the fact that
they are much lighter in character than either the "English
Suites" or the "German Suites"--and rather more akin in
spirit to the suites of Couperin and the other French mast-
ers--is believed to be the probable reason for the nickname.

210   "La Frescobalda"
      Girolamo Frescobaldi (arr Segovia).    Aria with Varia-
      tions

      The guitarist Andrés Segovia arranged this Aria with
Variations, credited to Frescobaldi, for guitar.    The three
variations include a gagliarda and a fast dance.    The theme
is repeated at the end.    Because Segovia took this theme
and variations from Frescobaldi he subtitled the work "La
Frescobalda. "

211   "The Frog" [Der Frosch]
      Haydn.    String Quartet, op. 50 no. 6, in D major
      (Hob. III, 49)

In the rather serious and thoughtful Op. 50 there is
one quartet filled with Haydn's particular sense of humor.
It is No. 6 of the set, popularly called "The Frog. " The
Finale has many gay croaking sounds produced by playing
the same notes alternately on two neighboring strings.


212   "From My Life" [Aus meinem Lebel; Z mého života]
      Bedřich Smetana.   String Quartet No. 1 in E minor

      Bedřich Smetana himself supplied a complete program
for this work which explains his subtitle.   The four movements depict the "romantic tendency and unsatisfied yearn-
ings of his early life. "
      The first movement is restless; the second, a
charming polka, showing the lighter side of his youthful
life; the third, a beautiful sustained slow movement ("the
bliss of my first love for my wife"); and the fourth, a lively finale: "the discovery of how to treat the national material in music. "   However, a note of sadness creeps into the
last movement:   "the beginning of my deafness, a glimpse
into the melancholy future. "   A somber tremolo in the lower instruments gives this ominous feeling.


213   "From the New World" [Z Nového Světa]
      Dvořák.   Symphony in E minor op. 95 [old no. 5,
      new no. 9] (Burghauser 178)

      The most important composition that Dvořák wrote dur-
ing his first American period, when he was director of the
National Conservatory in New York, was the famous Symphony in E minor nicknamed "From the New World. "   It is
not, as many supposed, a symphonic elaboration of actual
Negro and Indian themes, but merely a reflection of their
spirit and structural characteristics.
      When the symphony was performed in Berlin in
1900, Dvořák is said to have written to the conductor, Os-
kar Nedbal, "I sent you Kretzschmar's analysis of the Symphony but omit that nonsense about my having made use of
Indian and American motives.   That is a lie; I tried to
write only in the spirit of those national American melodies. "
      The marvelous popular Largo of this symphony is
partly inspired by some episodes of Longfellow's Hiawatha,
but it also reflects Dvořák's reminiscences of his home in
Bohemia and his loneliness in a distant land, a "new world"
to him indeed.

214  "Der Frosch"  (see "The Frog")
     Haydn.  String Quartet, op. 50 no. 6, in D major
     (Hob. III, 49)


215  "Der Frühling"  (see "Spring Sonata")
     Beethoven.  Sonata for Violin and Piano, op. 24, in
     F major


216  "Der Frühling"  (see "Spring Symphony")
     Schumann.  Symphony, op. 38 no. 1, in B♭ major


217  "Frühlings Quintet"  (see "Spring Quintet")
     Brahms.  String Quintet, op. 88, in F major


218  "Frühlingslied" (see "Spring Song")
     Mendelssohn.  Piece for Piano, op. 62 no. 6, in A
     major


219  "Für Elise"
     Beethoven.  Bagatelle for Piano in A minor   (WoO 59)

     The bagatelle subtitled "Für Elise" was written on Ap-
ril 25, 1810, and was discovered many years later by
Beethoven's first biographer, Ludwig Nohl, in the estate of
a friend, Therese Malfatti, whom Beethoven intended to
marry.   Nohl misread the dedication, "für Therese, am 27
April zur Erinnerung an L. v. Bthvn. "   Poor Therese,
Beethoven did not marry her, and the millions who know
this charming little piece call it by a meaningless name.


220  "Funeral March"  (see "Song Without Words")
     Mendelssohn.  Piece for Piano, op. 62 no. 3, in E
     minor


221  "Funeral March"
     Chopin.  Prelude, op. 28 no. 20, in C minor  (Brown
     123, no. 21)

     Each of the Op. 28 preludes of Chopin was given a
subtitle by Hans von Bülow, who describes this one thus:

"A funeral procession moves slowly through a park; now it has disappeared under the trees (pp); now the moon shines upon it (the upper voice must be played with particular brightness and distinctness).   It turns a corner; the figures are now seen only as shadows against the wall, where they appear magnified to twice their size.   Suddenly a deep black shadow covers the wall (final C minor chord)--it is the coffin! " [Musician, xvi (1911)].


222   "Funeral March Sonata"
      Beethoven.   Sonata for Piano, op. 26, in A♭ major

According to tradition, the second movement of this sonata, the "Marcia Funebre sulla Morte d'un Eroe" ("funeral march on the death of a hero"), which gives the sonata its nickname, was inspired by the funeral march in a very popular opera by Ferdinand Paër.   The latter was a young composer of the day who had produced a series of popular works on the court stage.   As he was working in a sphere totally different from that of Beethoven, there was no rivalry between them and their relations were cordial and friendly. Beethoven was supposed to have gone to the theatre with Paër to hear one of his operas and the funeral march in it was the inspiration for the Funeral March of the Sonata Op. 26.


223   "Funeral March Sonata"
      Chopin.   Sonata for Piano, op. 35, in B♭ minor
      (Brown 120)

It is the slow movement, entitled "Marche Funèbre," of this sonata that has given it its nickname.


224   "Funeral Ode" [Trauerode]
      J. S. Bach.   Lass Fürstin lass noch einen Strahl--
      Cantata 198   (BWV 198)

When Queen Christiane Eberhardine died on September 7, 1727, all Saxony mourned for her.   This cantata was commissioned by the rector for the memorial ceremony in St. Paul's Church, and is thus usually known by its subtitle.

225   "Funeral Symphony"  (see "Trauer Symphonie")
      Haydn.  Symphony No. 44 in E minor  (Hob. I, 44)


226   "Funeral Waltz"  (see "Trauerwalzer")
      Schubert.  Waltz, op. 9 no. 2  (D. 365, No. 2)


227   "Gaelic Symphony"
      Mrs. H. H. A. Beach.  Symphony op. 32 in E minor

      In the third movement the solo violin has a melody of
strong Gaelic character with a characteristic Celtic closing
cadence.  And although the melody in the second movement
is entitled "alla siciliana" it easily could be an Irish song.
Some believe that the Gaelic character suffuses the entire
symphony.


228   "La Gaieté"
      Chopin.  Polonaise for Piano and Cello in C major,
         op. 3  (Brown 41)


229   "Il Gardellino"  (see "The Bullfinch")
      Vivaldi.  Concerto for Flute and Strings, op. 10 no. 3,
         in D major  (F. VI, 14); and Concerto in D major
         for Flute, Oboe, Violin, Bassoon and Continuo  (F.
         XII, 9)


230   "Der Gassenhauer"  (see "Street Song")
      Beethoven.  Trio for Clarinet, Cello and Piano, op. 11


231   "Geister Trio"  (see "The Ghost Trio")
      Beethoven.  Trio for Piano, Violin and Cello, op. 70,
         in D major


232   "The German Michel"  [Der deutsche Michel]
      Bruckner.  Symphony No. 8 in C minor

      The subtitle was given to this symphony by Bruckner
with particular reference to the Scherzo movement.  The
composer felt that the principal theme of this movement
pictured the stubborn hardheaded Austrian peasant, who was

often nicknamed "Michel. " In a letter to Helm, the critic,
Bruckner wrote: "My Michel typifies the Austrian folk
spirit, the idealistic dreamer, one who would pull his cap
over his ears and cry 'Punch away, I can stand it'. "

233   "A German Requiem" [Ein deutsches Requiem]
      Brahms.   For Soloists, Chorus and Orchestra, op. 45

      According to Grove's Dictionary the subtitle is a faulty
English term still used for Brahms' Requiem op. 45.   The
original title, "Ein deutsches Requiem," simply means "a
requiem in German" and is therefore meaningless when sung
in any other language.   Brahms really wanted only to indicate that he was using appropriate words selected from the
German Bible instead of those of the Roman liturgy.   However, the work is constantly referred to as "A German
Requiem. "

234   "German Suites" [Klavierübung, Teil I]
      J. S. Bach.   Six Partitas for Piano:   no. 1 B♭ major;
      no. 2 C minor; no. 3 A minor; no. 4 D major; no.
      5 G major; no. 6 E minor   (BWV 825-830)

      There are at least two conjectures as to the reason
these partitas were nicknamed "German Suites. "   First, by
analogy, since the other sets had been nicknamed "French"
and "English," and second, because Bach's own designation
"Partien" (a purely German term) suggested that the composer himself regarded them as conforming in style to the
German tradition.

235   "Gesangscene"
      Louis Spohr.   Concerto for Violin No. 8 in A minor

      Spohr was a violinist and composer who lived from
1784-1859.   His whole school of playing was to make the
violin sing and to conceal the means by which good music
was produced.   This concerto was written in 1816 and to
humor the opera loving public of Italy, Spohr subtitled it
"Gesangscene" or "In Modo d'una scena cantante" ("in the
fashion of a vocal scena").   The concerto imitates the three-
part operatic aria, although it is written in one movement.
The three sections suggest the recitativo, air and cabaletta.

236  "Gettysburg Address Symphony"
      Roy Harris.  Symphony No. 6

    Roy Harris was born on Lincoln's birthday and in a log
cabin.  David Ewen has commented, "The shadow of Abe
Lincoln has hovered over Harris's life since childhood.
The sixth symphony reflects the composer's great admiration for and spiritual affinity with the great Emancipator"
[World of 20th Century Music, p. 342].  The symphony
draws its program from the Gettysburg Address.


237  "The Ghost Trio"  [Geister-Trio]
      Beethoven.  Trio for Piano, Violin and Cello, op. 70,
          in D major

    It is the weird figure of the second movement that has
given the trio its nickname.  According to Nottebohm, the
figure appears among Beethoven's sketches for the opening
scene of the witches in Macbeth.  Apparently he still had
this scene in mind when he wrote the trio and he increased
the eerie effect by giving the piano light tremolo chords
and mysterious chromatic scales.


238  "Giant Fugue"  [Klavierübung, Teil III]
      J. S. Bach.  Fugue for Organ in D minor (choral
          prelude on the creed "Wir Glauben All")  (BWV 680)

    The nickname was given to this piece by George Coop-
er, the London organist, who did much to popularize Bach's
organ music in England.  Undoubtedly, the stalking figure
in the bass was the inspiration for it.  Harvey Grace in his
book, The Organ Works of Bach, says, "The ground bass is
obviously intended to typify faith and the less we think of a
giant walking upstairs and tumbling down again, the better"
[p. 215].


239  "The Giant Symphony"  [Riesen-Symphonie]
      Mahler.  Symphony No. 5 in C♯ minor

    Immediately after the premiere of this symphony by
the Gürzenich Orchestra in Cologne on October 18, 1904,
several critics nicknamed it "The Giant Symphony."  This
was undoubtedly so because of its huge dimensions and the
extraordinary size of the orchestra called for in the score.

Of course these critics could not know that it was to be followed in a few years by the Eighth Symphony, a work of
much larger proportions which was to be nicknamed "The
Symphony of A Thousand. "


240  "Gmunden-Gastein"
     Schubert.  Symphony in C major  (D. 849)

In the year 1825 Schubert and his friend Vogl took a
pleasure trip to Gmunden and Gastein, two beautiful spots
in Upper Austria.  It was during the trip that Schubert
wrote this C major Symphony.
     Unfortunately the symphony is now lost and during
the centenary year of Schubert's birth, the Columbia Gramo-
phone Company offered a reward of £400 for its discovery,
but it was never found.  Sometimes the C major Symphony
is referred to as "Gastein" but Otto Erich Deutsch, in The
Schubert Reader [p. 454], says: "Since Schubert wrote the
D major pianoforte Sonata op. 53 at Gastein during August,
1825, it is hardly credible that the lost Symphony long
known as the 'Gastein' Symphony also originated there.  The
fact is that it was merely finished there, so that it would
be much better called the 'Gmunden Gastein' or better still
the 'Lost Symphony'. "
     It is believed that the Grand Duo, a four-hand piece
for piano, is an arrangement of this C major Symphony.


241  "Goin' Home"
     Dvořák.  Largo of Symphony "From the New World"
     in E minor, op. 95  (Burghauser 178)

Words were set to this movement by William Arms
Fisher in 1922, and it is sung under the popular title of
"Goin' Home" [see James Fuld, Book of World Famous
Music, p. 454].


242  "Goldberg Variations"
     J. S. Bach.  Aria with Thirty Variations  (BWV 988)

The original title of this work is "Aria mit verschie-
denen Veränderungen vors Clavicembal mit zwei Manualer"
("aria with different variations for the harpsichord with two
manuals").  The Russian Ambassador to the court of Dresden, Count Hermann Karl von Kayserling, suffering from

insomnia, always had famous instrumentalists attached to
his service, who could play for him during his sleepless
nights.

At one time, J. Theodor Goldberg, a brilliant harpsichordist, and the best pupil of Bach, was engaged to fill
this position.   Count Kayserling asked Bach to write a piece
which Goldberg might play for him during his sieges of insomnia.

Bach set to work with a great deal of enthusiasm,
and while searching for a theme on which to build some
variations, found in his wife's notebook a Sarabande in G
major whose ground bass attracted him, and he made it the
basis of the 30 variations.   A short time later he sent Kayserling the monumental "Goldberg Variations" and Kayserling, in turn, sent Bach a snuff box filled with 100 louis
d'or as a token of his appreciation.


243   "Golden Sonata"
      Purcell.   Sonata No. 9 in F major   (Zimmerman 810)

This sonata, which is one of a set of ten sonatas for
strings and continuo, is one of Purcell's larger works, consisting of an opening movement, a large canzona, grave and
Allegro.   The movements are all very well constructed and
quite distinct from one another in character, but it is difficult to know why No. 9 has been "crowned" above the others as the "Golden Sonata."   The title dates from 1704.


244   "Gossips at the Coffee Table" [Der Kaffeeklatsch]
      Haydn.   Number 18 of Set of Pieces for Musical
         Clocks   (Hob. XIX, 6)

This is one of a set of pieces that Haydn wrote for
musical clocks.   Niemecz, Prince Esterházy's librarian,
built the clocks and Haydn provided the music for them.
When Haydn presented Florian Gassmann, the Austrian court
conductor, with one of these clocks, his family nicknamed
the piece it played, "Gossips at the Coffee Table."


245   "Gothique"
      Charles Marie Widor.   Symphony No. 9, op. 70, in
         C major   (Organ)

It is because the composer attempted to describe in

tone the style of Gothic architecture that he subtitled his
symphony so.   The first performance was given by Widor
at the opening ceremony celebrating the rebuilding of the
organ at St. Orien.


246   "La Gracieuse"
      Chopin.   Ballade for Piano in F major, op. 38
      (Brown 102)


247   "Gran Partita"
      Mozart.   Serenade [for wind instruments] No. 10 in
      B♭ major   (K. 361)

   This work has the subtitle "Gran Partita" indicated in
Köchel's catalogue as a superscription (Überschrift) over the
manuscript score.   This can probably be explained by the
length of the work which has seven movements and takes 45
minutes to play.
      According to John N. Burk in his Mozart and His
Music, "No other master could have detained an audience so
long in this constricted medium without causing a weary
sense of repetition; Mozart's score gives a sense of fresh
disclosure to the very end" [p. 311].


248   "Grand Concerto"
      Henri Vieuxtemps.   Concerto for Violin in D minor,
      No. 4


249   "Grand Rondeau"
      Schubert.   Rondo for Piano Four Hands, op. 104, in
      A major   (D. 951)

   The Rondo in A major was published posthumously by
Artaria with the subtitle, "Grand Rondeau." According to
Alfred Einstein, in his Schubert: A Musical Portrait, "This
Rondo says in unpretenious Viennese language what the slow
movement of C major Symphony expresses with intense
gravity and slightly all'ongarese" [p. 282].


250   "Grand Sonata"
      Beethoven.   Sonata for Piano No. 4, op. 7, in E♭
      major

The piece was published in October 1797, alone as a "Grand Sonata. " The longer lines and development of the first movement and the great brilliance of the Rondo movement made Beethoven feel that the sonata was a piece of concert stature, hence the subtitle, "Grand Sonata. "

251  "Grande Sonate"
     Schubert.  Sonata for Piano, op. 143, in A minor
     (D. 784)

In February 1823 Schubert wrote a Piano Sonata in A minor and dedicated it to Felix Mendelssohn.  This was published posthumously in 1839 by Diabelli as Op. 143 and subtitled by him, "Grande Sonate. " Alfred Einstein, in his book, Schubert, A Musical Portrait, says, "Yet it is anything but a 'Grande Sonate' in the Beethoven sense of word.  In spite of its strange manner and explosive outbursts, it is an intimate sonata contenting itself with three movements and modest dimensions" [p. 215].

252  "Grandes Etudes de Paganini"
     Liszt.  Six Studies Transcribed from Paganini's Violin
     Caprices

The so called "Grandes Etudes de Paganini," or sometimes merely "Paganini Studies," are six brilliant piano studies that Liszt transcribed from Paganini's Caprices for the Violin.  They are:  No. 1 G minor; No. 2 E♭ major; No. 3 G♯ minor (also known as "La Campanella"); No. 4 E major; No. 5 E major; and No. 6 A minor.

253  "Gratulations Menuett"
     Beethoven.  Allegretto for Orchestra in E♭ major
     (WoO 3)

In October 1822, a week after the performance of Beethoven's Overture, "Consecration of the House, " the composer wrote what Bäverle's Theaterzeitung called a glorious new symphony, but what really was the E♭ Allegretto nicknamed "Gratulations Menuett. " This was written and performed as a surprise for the nameday of Hensler, director of the Josephstadt Theatre, who was a great friend of Beethoven.
          The autograph had the following inscription: "Tempo

di minuetto quasi allegretto.    Allegretto non troppo, " but
this was scratched out by Beethoven and "Gratulations
Menuett" was written in its place.


254   "Grazer-Fantasie"
      Schubert.   For  Piano,  C major   (not in Deutsch)

      In 1968 the Internationales Schubert Institut in Tübin-
gen, Germany, undertook the publication of Schubert's complete works.   In the search for manuscripts, letters and
documents, Konrad Stekl, a musicologist and composer living in Graz, was asked to check on possible papers regarding Schubert's relationship with Joseph Hüttenbrenner, who
had lived in that area.   Through the widow of a great neph-
ew of Hüttenbrenner he was able to go through a chest
containing papers and various compositions by Schubert
which had been stored in her attic.
      Among these was this Fantasie for Piano.   Although
the manuscript was not in Schubert's own hand, experts
have testified as to its authenticity and an announcement of
its discovery was issued.   Bärenreiter Verlag in Kassel
Germany arranged to publish this work and it was nicknamed "Grazer-Fantasie. "   It is thought to have been written in 1818 when Schubert was almost 20 years old.   It
had its first performance in the United States on November
2, 1969 on Columbia Broadcasting System "Camera III"
television program performed by pianist Lili Kraus.
      Harold Schonberg, music critic of the New York
Times, wrote that even though it was a youthful work the
Fantasie revealed an opening theme that nobody but Schubert
could have composed.   However, its authenticity was ques-
tioned by J. F. Vogel (in Die Musikforschung, 24, 1971,
168-72).


255   "Great"
      Purcell.   Chaconne for Two Violins, Viola da Gamba
      or Cello, in G minor   (Zimmerman 807)

      This chaconne is the entire sixth sonata from the son-
atas in four parts published by Purcell's widow in 1797.
These sonatas were written for two violins, a bass line
which could be performed by viola da gamba or cello, and
a keyboard figured bass.   This chaconne has particularly
rich harmonic effects and perhaps this is why it has been
nicknamed "Great. "

256   "The Great"
      J. S. Bach.    Fantasie and Fugue for Organ in G minor
      (BWV 542)

This Fantasie and Fugue in G minor, sometimes called
Prelude and Fugue, was written by Bach for performance in
Hamburg, when he visited that city in 1720.  It is very
likely that the subject of the fugue was chosen from one of
Reinken's works to humor the old organist.   Undoubtedly the
great expressiveness of the music of the Fantasie and Fugue
plus the wonderful daring of the harmonic structure have
given it the nickname "The Great. "

257   "The Great"
      Mozart.   Mass in C minor   (K.  427)

This mass owes its origin to a vow made by Mozart
during an illness of Constanze Weber in which he promised to
write a mass if she would recover and become his wife.  He
wanted to please his bride with effective soprano solos displaying her range, and at the same time increase his family's respect for her.   Their planned first visit to Salzburg
was postponed and actually they were married on August 4,
1782, before the mass had been completed.
        The first performance of the Mass was finally given
in Salzburg in the church of St.  Peter on August 25, 1783
and Constanze sang the soprano part.   The reason for the
nickname "The Great" is that this mass exceeded anything
Mozart had done both in length and performing forces.   He
scored it for solo voices; oboes, bassoons, horns and
trumpets in pairs; four trombones (used independently as
well as to double the choral parts); strings (including violas); and organ.   He also used a double chorus for the
second time in his life, the first being the "Offertorium"
(K.  260).

258   "The Great"
      Schubert.   Symphony No.  7 in C major   (D.  944)

The Symphony in C major is chronologically Schubert's
ninth and last symphony because it was written in the last
year of his life, but owing to the fact that it was published
before the "Unfinished" it is known as the seventh.   Schubert had submitted the symphony to the Vienna Philharmonic
Society shortly after completing it but it was refused on the

grounds that it was "too long and difficult. " These very
impressive dimensions are what gave it the nickname
"Great. "

Some years later when Robert Schumann moved to
Vienna he not only visited Schubert's grave but also visited
Schubert's brother, Ferdinand. During this visit, on January 1, 1839, Schumann discovered this great C major Symphony among a pile of manuscripts. In his celebrated review of it he referred to it as the symphony of "Heavenly
Lengths" and went on to say, "Deep down in this Symphony
there lies more than mere song, more than mere joy and
sorrow, as already expressed in music in a hundred other
instances; it transports us into a world where we cannot recall ever having been before. "

259   "Great Fugue" (see "Grosse Fuge")
      Beethoven.  String Quartet, op. 133, in B♭ major


260   "Great Mass"
      Bruckner.  Mass No. 3 in F minor

The Mass No. 3 in F is generally considered the best
of Bruckner's three major masses. It is because of the
outstanding musical qualities as well as its great orchestral
scope and dimensions that it has received its subtitle.


261   "Great Mass with Organ" ⌈Grosse Orgel-Messe⌋
      Haydn.  Mass in E♭ major  (Hob. XII, 4)

In this mass, a composition on a large scale, Haydn
was much more interested in the musical possibilities of
the work than in the interpretation of the text.

It calls for a four-part chorus, four solo singers,
string instruments, two English horns, trumpets, horns and
an obbligato organ part. The organ part is embellished with
brilliant runs and ornaments which make the nickname quite
understandable.


262   "The Great Quartets" (see "Sun Quartets")
      Haydn.  String Quartets, op. 20  (Hob. III, 31-36)


263   "Grenadier"
      Haydn.  March No. 6 in E♭ major  (Hob. VIII, 6)

264   "Grief"   (see "L'Intimité")
      Chopin.   Etude, op. 10 no. 3, in E major   (Brown
      74)


265   "Grosse Fuge" [Great Fugue]
      Beethoven.   String Quartet, op. 133, in B♭ major

      The "Grosse Fuge" which Beethoven intended as the
finale or a sixth movement to the quartet in B♭, Op. 130,
would have made the work too long for contemporary listening ability.   When Artaria offered to publish the fugue separately Beethoven reluctantly consented.   The subtitle comes
from the greatness and complexity of the music.   Actually
there are three fugues built upon a single theme and bound
by an introduction and a coda.


266   "Die grossen Quartetten"   (see "Sun Quartets")
      Haydn.   String Quartets, op. 20   (Hob. III, 31-36)


267   "Guggenheim Jeune"
      Virgil Thomson.   Sonata for Keyboard No. 4

      The composer wrote the following concerning this work:
"My keyboard sonata number 4 is literally a portrait of
Miss Peggy Guggenheim.   At the time it was made she was
planning to open an art gallery in New York and call it
Guggenheim Jeune (after the Paris dealer, Bernheim Jeune).
This was, if you wish, a nickname for her."


268   "Gypsy Trio"
      Haydn.   Trio for Piano, Violin and Cello No. 1 in G
      major   (Hob. XV, 25)

      It is because of the high-spirited "Rondo all'ongarese"
in the Finale movement that the trio has received its nickname.   This has been arranged for piano and is extremely
popular in that form.


269   "Hades"
      Chopin.   Prelude, op. 28 no. 16, in B♭ minor
      (Brown 107, no. 16)

Each of the Op. 28 preludes of Chopin was given a
subtitle by Hans von Bülow.  Of this one he comments,
"Another hallucination such as his excited fancy often con-
jured up.  An abyss opens before his eyes; from it devils
emerge, each one chasing the other in mighty leaps (the
left hand embraces nearly the whole extent of the keyboard).
One by one they begin to sink into the depths, when at the
stretto ensues a scuffle, all try to descend at the same
time,  We notice one in particular who rises and falls alternately; all at once (C flat) he leaps into air and falls into the pit, followed by all the others.  The gulf closes"
[Musician, xvi (1911)].


270  "Haffner March"
     Mozart.  March in D major  (K. 249)

This march was so nicknamed because it began the
"Haffner Symphony" in its original version.


271  "Haffner Serenade"
     Mozart.  Serenade No. 7 in D major  (K. 250)

Siegmund Haffner was a wealthy fellow townsman (Salzburg) of Mozart's father.  When his daughter, Elizabeth,
was to be married, Mozart was asked to provide music for
the gala ceremony.
     The Serenade No. 7 was the music Mozart wrote
for the wedding reception, and thus its nickname.  It was a
long piece of seven movements and if it had been played
continuously would have lasted an hour.  It is not known
how the music was spaced, but it is to be hoped, in view
of the many quiet portions, that there was less "music
drowning chatter" than there is at wedding receptions today.


272  "Haffner Symphony"
     Mozart.  Symphony in D major  (K. 385)

This symphony was composed for the Haffner family of
Salzburg, probably in honor of the ennoblement of the young-
er Siegmund Haffner, July 24, 1782.  Mozart composed it
in great haste and sent it piecemeal to Salzburg.  The work
was at first intended to be another serenade, for it originally contained two minuets and began with a march, but after
several changes it took on the form of a four-movement

symphony and was first performed in Vienna on March 23, 1783.


273   "Halle Sonatas"
      Handel.  Three Sonatas for Flute and Harpsichord

In volume 48 of the complete edition of Handel, Chrysander writes the following concerning the three flute sonatas of the young Handel: "It is possible that these compositions for the flute originated in Halle, hence the subtitle.  Knowledge of them, however, may not have extended any farther until about 1710 from Hanover.  The cavaliers of that court were zealous flutists and through them the compositions may have found their way later on as far as England. "


274   "Hallelujah"
      Handel.  Concerto for Organ, op. 9, in B♭ major

Handel, in writing new compositions, would very often borrow material that he had already used in previous music. In the first movement of this organ concerto he used the opening phrase of his "Hallelujah Chorus" many times and that is the obvious reason for the nickname.


275   "Hamburger Sonate"
      C. P. E. Bach.  Sonata for Flute and Piano in G major   (Wotquenne 133)

It is believed that Carl Philipp Emanuel Bach wrote this sonata in Hamburg and that is why it is known as the "Hamburger Sonate. "


276   "Hammerklavier"
      Beethoven.  Sonata for Piano, op. 106, in B♭ major

The nickname commonly given to this sonata could just as well have been given to the Sonata Op. 101 which was also published as "für das Hammerklavier. "
      It seems that the suggestion had been made for German composers to substitute German terms in music in place of Italian ones.  With characteristic impetuosity, Beethoven decided to reform at once.  Actually it was the

Sonata Op. 101 that Beethoven wrote to his publisher, Stein-
er, about, even though it meant re-engraving the title page.
　　　He wrote to him in his newly assumed "military
style. "
　　　"To the Well born Lieut[enant] Gen[eral] for his
own hands / Publicandum... / After individual examination
and taking the advice of my Counsel we have determined and
hereby determine that hereafter on all our works with German titles Hammerklavier be printed in place of pianoforte.... "


277　"Harmoniemesse" (see "Wind Band Mass")
　　　Haydn.　Mass in B♭ major　(Hob. XXII, 14)


278　"The Harmonious Blacksmith"
　　　Handel.　Air and Variations for Harpsichord

　　　This is the air and variations from Handel's fifth harpsichord suite and he gave it no special title.　There is no
foundation for the story that Handel heard the air sung by a
blacksmith at Edgware, near London.　"The Edgware Blacksmith" story was first told by the notoriously inventive
Richard Clark in his reminiscences of Handel, written in
1836.
　　　In 1889, in the first edition of Grove's Dictionary
of Music, the following appeared, written by William Chap-
pell.　"A few months after Clark's publication, the writer
saw the late J. W. Winsor of Bath, a great admirer of
Handel, and one who knew all his published works.　He told
the writer that the story of the Blacksmith of Edgware was
pure imagination, that the original publisher of Handel's
music was a music seller at Bath named Lintern, whom he
knew personally from buying music at his shop, that he had
asked Lintern the reason for this new name, and had been
told that it was a nickname given to himself, because he
had been brought up as a blacksmith, and later turned to
music, and this was the piece he was constantly asked to
play.　He printed this in a separate form, because he was
able to sell many more copies" [quoted in Scholes, Oxford
Companion to Music, p. 685].
　　　There is still another story about the naming of this
composition:　while Handel was engaged at the town of
Canons, near Edgware, he wrote a suite of pieces for the
harpsichord, containing the famous "Air and Variations. "
The work was published without any title, and for a hundred

years no one thought of connecting it with an anvil, blacksmith or a thunderstorm.  The title was first attached to
the work about 1820, when a publisher in Bath gave it this
name because a blacksmith's apprentice was always whistling
the air.
       The legend of the Edgware blacksmith originated
about 1835, to be followed by the discovery of an "actual"
anvil at Whitchurch, and an erection of a memorial to the
"actual" blacksmith.


279   "The Harp of the Poet"   (see "Songs Without Words")
      Mendelssohn.   Piece for Piano, op. 38 no. 3, in E
      major


280   "Harp Quartet"
      Beethoven.   String Quartet, op. 74, in E♭ major

       The nickname for this quartet is derived from two
short passages in the first movement with pizzicato arpeggios ascending through the three lower parts, in one case
to lead to the recapitulation and in the other to form the
coda.   The effect is that of a harp, and according to Ulrich, in his Chamber Music, "The unfortunate nickname has
drawn more attention to those passages than they deserve"
[p. 271].


281   "Haydn Quartets"
      Mozart.   String quartets  (K. 387, 421, 428, 458,
      464, 465)

       On January 15, 1785, Mozart invited Haydn to hear
these six string quartets which he had written for and dedicated to his older friend.   Mozart, in his famous dedicatory
letter in the first edition issued, in September 1785, by
Artaria, described the works as follows "essi sono, è vero,
il frutto di una lunga e laboriosa fatica. "
       These quartets represent a living testimony to the
friendship between the two composers, and the works have
always been known as the "Haydn Quartets. "


282   "Heartfelt Happiness"
      Chopin.   Prelude, op. 28 no. 19, in E♭ major
      (Brown 107, no. 19)

Each of the Op. 28 preludes of Chopin was given a
subtitle by Hans von Bülow.  He wrote of this piece, "The
ecstasy pictured embraces the entire instrument with a
mighty grasp; an unwonted extension of the harmonies in
each hand seems to give them exceptional force and impres-
siveness, the joy they express knows no bounds; the whole
horizon is irradiated with rapture ineffable.  With the diminished sevenths the enraptured one begins to feel some uncertainty; he loses the thread, resumes the former melody,
and in spite of various harmonic detours remains in E flat.
A slight doubt (C and C flat) is silenced (piano); a final
deviation to A major leads back to the original key and to
former happiness" [Musician, xvi (1911)].


283   "Hebrew Rhapsody for Cello and Orchestra"
      Bloch.   Schelomo

This piece has been given its subtitle because in it
Bloch tries to portray, as he himself says, "The Jewish
soul with its complexity, its ardour and its agitation which
I feel vibrating throughout the Bible, the freshness and
simplicity of the Patriarchs, the vehemence expressed by
the Prophets, the love for Justice, the despair of Ecclesi-
astes, the pain and depth of the Book of Job, the sensuality
of the Song of Songs.... "


284   "Heiliger Dankgesang"
      Beethoven.   String Quartet in A minor, op. 132

The sketches of the A minor Quartet date back to 1824,
but Beethoven's severe illness in the spring of 1825 interrupted the work.  His consequent recovery was the inspiration for the slow movement of the quartet which he titled
"Heiliger Dankgesang eines Genesenen an die Gottheit, in
der lydischen Tonart" ("holy song of thanksgiving to the
Divinity by a convalescent, in the Lydian mode").  Out of
this came the nickname.


285   "Heiligmesse"  (see "Holy Mass")
      Haydn.   Mass in B♭ major (Missa Sancti Bernardi de
         Offida)  (Hob. XXII, 10)


286   "The Hen"  [La Poule]
      Haydn.   Symphony No. 83 in G minor  (Hob. I, 83)

This is the second of the so-called Paris Symphonies of Haydn. The nickname is derived from the clucking effect of the woodwind accompaniment to the second subject of the first movement.

287 "Hero"
Beethoven. String Quartet, op. 59 no. 3, in C major

The C major, the third of the Rasumovsky Quartets (q. v.), is sometimes called the "Hero." This probably originates from the Finale of the quartet, which is the culmination of the whole of Op. 59. It is as though Beethoven felt like a hero to himself in being able to conquer his dreadful thoughts of suicide. The music is filled with the unrestrained joy of the ecstasy of being alive.

288 "Hexenmenuett" (see "Witches Minuet")
Haydn. Minuet of String Quartet, op. 76 no. 2, in D
minor (Hob. III, 76)

289 "Historical Symphony"
Louis Spohr. Symphony No. 6, op. 116, in G major

Spohr wrote his "Historical Symphony" in the style and taste of four different periods of musical history. The first period is that of 1720, that of Bach and Handel; the second, Haydn and Mozart, 1780; the third, Beethoven, 1820; and the fourth, the most modern period, 1840.

290 "Holy Mass" [Heiligmesse]
Haydn. Mass in B♭ major (Missa Sancti Bernadi de
Offida) (Hob. XXII, 10)

This mass is called "Heiligmesse" ("holy mass") in Germany because of the use of the hymn "Heilig, heilig" by the contralto and tenor in the Sanctus. The mass was composed in 1796 and dedicated to the memory of the monk Bernardus von Offida, who had been canonized in the previous year.

291 "Homage to Boccherini"
Castelnuovo-Tedesco. Sonata for Guitar

"Homage to Boccherini" was written at a request from
the great guitar virtuoso, Segovia.   The latter suggested
that the composer write a complete sonata as homage to
his countryman, Luigi Boccherini.   Castelnuovo-Tedesco
feels that it is only in the Minuet and perhaps the first
movement that the subtitle "Homage to Boccherini" is appropriate.


292   "Homelessness"   (see "Songs Without Words")
      Mendelssohn.   Piece for Piano, op. 10 no. 1, in E
      minor


293   "Les Hommages"
      Nicolas Nabokov.   Concerto for Cello and Orchestra

      Nabokov has given the following information about this
work which he wrote in 1951-1952.   "I have called it 'Les
Hommages' because it is dedicated to the memory or rather
to reminiscenses of melodies by Tchaikovsky ('Serenata di
Pietro'), by Dargomijsky ('Ballata d'Alessandrio') and Glinka
('Corale di Michele').   Within the musical texture of both
the first and second movement are concealed bits of melodies by Tchaikovsky and Dargomijsky.   The listener may
make a game of trying to detect them.   The last movement
is a chorale on a famous theme by Glinka. "
      As a bit of a fantasy the composer has imagined
the cello as an elderly Russian baritone who is now a taxi
driver in Paris and who tried to recall parts of his beloved
repertoire of former days.   But his memory is a bit hazy
and all he can remember is the most obvious and the most
famous tidbits from his three favorite masters, Tchaikovsky,
Dargomijsky and Glinka.


294   "Hope"   (see "Songs Without Words")
      Mendelssohn.   Piece for Piano, op. 38 no. 4, in A
      major


295   "Horn-Signal" [Mit dem Hornsignal]
      Haydn.   Symphony No. 31 in D major   (Hob. I, 31)

      This symphony is known by still another nickname,
"Auf dem Aufstand" ("on the lookout"), which refers to that
moment before the chase where the hunter, lying in wait
for his quarry, first sights the long expected prey.   In this
symphony there are many solos for winds and particularly

for the four horns.  Not only does the first movement begin
with the characteristic horn call of the hunt, but it also
ends with it.


296    "Hornpipe Concerto"
       Handel.   Concerto Grosso No. 7 for Orchestra

        A hornpipe is a particular type of melody written in
Common Time, which was used to dance to.   Handel's
Seventh Concerto Grosso ends with a hornpipe and this is
why the nickname has been attached to it.


297    "The Horseman"   (see "The Rider")
       Haydn.   String quartet in G minor, op. 74 no. 3
       (Hob. III, 73)


298    "The House of the Devil" [La Casa del diavolo]
       Luigi Boccherini.   Symphony, op. 12 no. 4, in D mi-
       nor   (Gérard 506)

        According to Gérard, the popular title for this sym-
phony was found in Boccherini's autograph catalogue.   The
autograph MS. , formerly in Madrid in the archive of the
Boccherini family, was destroyed during the Spanish Civil
War.   "There are two copies of the score and parts in the
Milan Conservatorio, and both of these have the title 'La
Casa del diavolo'; in the absence of any autograph MS. it
may be used as an authority for the text" [Works of Boccherini, pp. 575-6].


299    "The House on Fire"   (see "The Frog")
       Haydn.   String Quartet, op. 50 no. 6, in D major
       (Hob. III, 49)


300    "How Do You Do? "
       Haydn.   Quartet, op. 33 no. 5, in G major   (Hob. III,
       41)

        The words "How Do You Do? " fit the first motive of the
quartet and, according to Percy Scholes, in the Oxford
Companion to Music [p. 687], this is the derivation of the
nickname.

301  "The Hunt"  (see no. 86, "La Chasse")
     Haydn.  String Quartet, op. 1 no. 1, in B♭ major
     (Hob. III, 1)


302  "The Hunt" [Der Jagd]
     Haydn.  Symphony No. 72 in D major  (Hob. I, 72)

This symphony has fallen into complete oblivion.  It
gives the impression of being a study for the "Horn-Signal
Symphony" [see entry 295], which has such a brilliant "hunting" orchestration.


303  "The Hunt" [La Chasse]
     Haydn.  Symphony No. 73 in D major  (Hob. I, 73)

In 1780 Haydn's new opera, La Fedeltà Premiata, was
produced at Esterháza.  The prelude to Act III was a brilliant hunting scene called "La Chasse" in which the oboes
and horns were used in sparkling rhythmic tunes.  Haydn
was very fond of this movement and not being willing to
have it die the swift death that was usually accorded to his
stage pieces, he wove it into a new symphony, No. 73,
which is known as "La Chasse."


304  "The Hunt" [Der Jagd]
     Mozart.  String Quartet in B♭ major  (K. 458)

The fourth of the so called "Haydn Quartets" has acquired this nickname because of the rollicking 6/8 rhythm
of its opening theme and the fanfare-like opening of the development.


305  "Hunting Song"  (see "Songs Without Words")
     Mendelssohn.  Piece for Piano, op. 19 no. 3, in A
        major


306  "Hymn of Praise" [Lobgesang]
     Mendelssohn.  Symphony No. 2 in B♭ major, op. 52,
        for Orchestra and Voices

This symphony, sometimes known as Cantata Op. 52,
derives its nickname from the second movement, which has

in it the famous hymn, "Nun danket alle Gott" ("Now thank
we all our God"). In the book, The Mendelssohn Family,
by Sebastian Hensel, Mendelssohn's sister, Fanny, wrote
that her brother composed this work for the festival of the
invention of printing.


307    "Hymnus Ambrosianus"
       Milhaud.  Symphony No. 3 for Chorus and Orchestra

    In The World of 20th Century Music [p. 638], David
Ewen has written that soon after the liberation of France
the French government commissioned Milhaud to write a Te
Deum to commemorate the event.  The composer decided
to extend the idea to symphonic proportions.  Because the
fourth movement was for chorus and orchestra he subtitled
it "Hymnus Ambrosianus. "


308    "Im Walde" [In the Forest]
       Joachim Raff.  Symphony No. 3 in F major, op. 153


309    "Image of America"
       Carl Eppert.  Symphony No. 7, in:  A Symphonic Cy-
          cle, op. 77

    The composer himself subtitled his symphony and also
subtitled each part as follows:  Prologue, "The Threshold";
Part I, "The Heritage"; Part II, "The Wilderness Trail";
and Part III, "The Vision. "


310    "Impatience"
       Chopin.  Prelude, op. 28 no. 22, in G minor  (Brown
          107, no. 22)

    Each of the Op. 28 preludes of Chopin was given a
subtitle by Hans von Bülow.  His commentary on this one
follows:  "(In this prélude no attention should be paid to the
bars which divide it into measures.)  An energetic melody
(as if representing a single person) begins in the bass and
presses forward impatiently; the right hand (the second person) accompanies it as if endeavoring to soothe it.  One
can hear the foot stamped (ff), the vexation increases; all
attempts at pacification are in vain, patience is exhausted
(chords of the diminished seventh); both of the dramatis

personae fling the doors angrily together" [Musician, xvi
(1911)].


311   "Imperial Mass"  (see "Nelson Mass")
      Haydn.   Mass in D minor  (Hob. XXII, 11)


312   "L'Impériale"
      Haydn.   Symphony No. 53 in D major  (Hob. I, 53)

     The history of Symphony No. 53 is complicated by the
fact that no one has been able to state exactly when it was
composed.   It is based upon an old French song and the
copy of the original chanson is included in the Wahl-Katalog,
a list of Haydn sources drawn up before World War I for
Breitkopf und Härtel by Dr. Wahl.
     As far as we know, the "Imperial Symphony" seems
in some way to be connected with a visit of the Empress
Maria Theresa to the castle of Esterháza when Haydn was
employed as court musician.


313   "In London Town"
      Elgar.   Overture, op. 40 (Cockaigne)

     When the overture was first performed by the Boston
Symphony Orchestra in November 1901, Philip Hale wrote
the following program notes which best explain the nickname
"In London Town":
     "The overture is a succession of scenes: it may
be called panoramic.   The scenes are connected by a slend-
er thread.   The composer imagines two lovers strolling
through the streets of the town.   The first picture suggested
is that of the animation of the intense vitality of the street
life.   Then comes a section, which, according to the composer's sketch, expresses the sincere and ardent spirit un-
derlying the Cockaigner's frivolity and luxury.
     "The lovers seek quiet in a park and give way to
their emotions.   They are interrupted and leave the park
and seek what Charles Lamb described as the 'sweet secur-
ity of the streets.'   A military band approaches, passes
with hideous rage and fury, and at last is at a safe and
reasonable distance.   The lovers go into a church.   The
organ is playing, and even here they cannot escape wholly
the noise of the street.   To the street they return, and the
former experiences are renewed. "

314    "In Memoriam"
       Gian Francesco Malipiero.    Symphony No. 4

On the occasion of the first performance of this symphony in Boston on February 27, 1948, the composer wrote
the following: "When Serge Koussevitsky commissioned my
fourth symphony for his Foundation, he could not have
chosen a more propitious moment for entrusting a musician
with the task of writing an elegy.   This terrible post-war
period is a huge cemetery in which is brought together all
that which is no more, so that one's soul has been disposed
to draw into itself and make its own the grief of a friend.
The dedication of this fourth symphony to the memory of
Natalie Koussevitsky is the best guide for listening to 'In
Memorian'. "


315    "In Memory of a Great Artist"
       Tchaikovsky.    Trio for Piano, Violin and Cello, op.
       50, in A major

In Modeste Tchaikovsky's biography of his brother
there is an interesting account of a walk in the country
taken by several professors at the Moscow Conservatory in
May 1873.    Among them were the great pianist, Nicolas
Rubinstein, and Peter Ilich Tchaikovsky.    During the walk,
Rubinstein gave the peasants food in exchange for their
singing and dancing folk tunes.    Tchaikovsky never forgot
this scene and when he wrote this trio, almost nine years
later, the memory of it suggested the theme of the second
movement.    The trio was inspired by the death of Nicolas
Rubinstein in 1881, just as Rachmaninoff's trio was inspired
by Tchaikovsky's death.


316    "In Modo Classico"
       Joseph Marx.    String Quartet in D major


317    "In the South" [Alassio]
       Elgar.    Overture, op. 50

The composer visited Alassio, an Italian seaport town
on the Mediterranean, near Genoa, and it was here that he
was supposed to have been inspired to write his Overture
Op. 50, which he himself subtitled.
       Sir Donald Francis Tovey, in his own inimitable

way, says: "I have not been to Alassio and so I cannot talk
of Elgar's special sources of inspiration for this brilliant
and sunshiny overture.   I only hope that if I ever do go
there I may not find myself in the position of the old lady
who said to Turner that she could not see in sunsets anything like his pictorial representations of them, to which of
course he replied 'Don't you wish you could?' If she could,
she would not have been able to find words for them; and if
ever I can see at places like Alassio what Elgar saw as he
saw it, I would much rather write a concert overture about
it than an analytical programme" [Essays in Musical Analysis, v. 6, p. 63].


318   "In Time of War"   (see "Kettledrum Mass")
      Haydn.   Mass in C major   (Hob. XXII, 9)


319   "Indian Lament"
      Dvořák.   Sonatina for Violin and Piano, op. 100

      According to Gervaise Hughes [Dvořák--His Life and
Music, p. 170], in October 1893 the composer made a few
sketches for an orchestral suite in D minor, one of which
incorporated a melody which he said to have jotted down on
his cuff when visiting the Minnehaha Falls near Minneapolis
early the previous month.   The project seems never to have
progressed beyond the embryo stage.   Dvořák used this
Minnehaha theme, however, as the basis of the slow movement of a sonatina for violin and piano which he completed
in November.   This was an intentionally unassuming little
work especially designed to be played by his 15-year-old
daughter, Ottilie, and his 10-year-old son, Antonín.   It is
because of his music of the Indian theme that it has been
nicknamed "Indian Lament."   Sometimes it is also called
"Indian Cradle Song" or "Indian Canzonetta."


320   "Indian Suite"
      MacDowell.   Suite No. 2, op. 48, in E minor

      MacDowell was inspired to subtitle his suite "Indian"
after reading Theodore Baker's book, Music of the North
American Indians.   In this suite the composer forms his
principal themes out of bits of Indian melodies, a harvest
song, a war song, a woman's dance of the Iroquois and a
love song of the Iowas.

MacDowell was contemporaneous with Dvořák in calling attention to the existence of native American music and it is interesting to note that the "Indian Suite" was fully sketched before Dvořák's "New World" Symphony appeared, although it did not get its first performance until three years later on January 23, 1896, by the Boston Symphony Orchestra in New York City.


321   "The Inextinguishable" [Det Udslukkelige]
      Carl Nielsen.   Symphony No. 4

Nielsen composed his Fourth Symphony, which he subtitled "The Inextinguishable," during World War I.   The music tries to give vent to Nielsen's feelings about the power of life to survive almost any catastrophe.   It is towards the end of the symphony, when all the clashing forces resolve themselves into two irreconcilable tonalities, that we get the real feeling of inextinguishableness.


322   "L'Inquietudine"
      Vivaldi.   Concerto for Violin, Strings and Harpsichord
      in D major   (F. I, 10)


323   "Intimate Pages" [Listy Duverné]
      Leoš Janáček.   String Quartet No. 2

The composer wrote this quartet as a devoted tribute to Mrs. Kamila Stossel, his loyal friend during the last decade of his life.   The Adagio in particular suggests nostalgic memories such as "Intimate Pages" are apt to evoke.


324   "L'Intimité" (also, "Grief")
      Chopin.   Etude, op. 10 no. 3, in E major   (Brown
      74)


325   "L'Invitation pour la danse"
      Chopin.   Waltz for Piano in E♭ major, op. 18
      (Brown 62)


326   "Irish"
      C. V. Stanford.   Symphony No. 3 in F minor, op. 28

327   "Italian Concerto"
      J. S. Bach.    Concerto in F major for Clavicembalo
      (BWV 971)

Bach wrote this F major Concerto for the two-manual
clavicembalo when he was very much interested in the Italian
instrumental style of Vivaldi and Albinoni.   It is because of
this influence that the concerto is known as the "Italian. "


328   "Italian Overture"
      Haydn.   Overture No. 4 in D major   (Hob. Ia, 4)

H. C. Robbins Landon, the important Haydn authority,
has an interesting comment on the subtitling of this overture:  it was "thought up by the recording company.   Grin-
nell of New York simply gave it a title because a title sells
better. "


329   "Italian Quartets"
      Mozart.   Seven String Quartets:  No. 1 in G major
      (K. 80); No. 2 in D major (K. 155); No. 3 in G
      major (K. 156); No. 4 in C major (K. 157); No. 5
      in F major (K. 158); No. 6 in B♭ major (K. 159);
      No. 7 in E♭ major (K. 160)

The seven so-called "Italian Quartets" were composed
when Mozart was a very young boy during his Italian travels.
The first one was composed in Lodi in 1770; the second,
probably in Bozen 1772; the third, in Milan in late 1772;
the fourth, in Milan in late 1772 or early 1773; the fifth,
in Milan in early 1773; the sixth, in Milan in early 1773;
and the seventh, in Milan in early 1773.
      They are all written in the Italian "taste," each
having three movements and usually omitting the minuets.
The young boy, the "Tedesco, " was eager to please the
Italian public and not mystify them.


330   "Italian Symphony"
      Mendelssohn.   Symphony No. 4, op. 90, in A major

The real feeling for Italy comes in the Finale movement of this symphony, the Saltarello.   It is said that when
Mendelssohn was visiting an old friend in Rome, Laura, his
young daughter and he delighted the composer by doing the

dance steps of the Saltarello for him.   The rhythm fascinated Mendelssohn and apparently came to his mind when he
was writing the symphony.
        Another incident which was said to have inspired the
symphony took place in front of the Inn at Amalfi, where the
young people were dancing.   In the middle of the dancing
Mendelssohn called out to a friend, "Oh, that melody, mark
it well.   You shall find it again in some shape or other in
a work of mine. "


331    "Der Jagd"   (see no. 86, "La Chasse")
       Haydn.   String Quartet, op. 1 no. 1, in B♭ major
       (Hob. III, 1)


332    "Der Jagd"   (see "The Hunt")
       Mozart.   String Quartet in B♭ major   (K. 458)


333    "Jagd-Sonate"   (see no. 83, "La Chasse")
       Beethoven.   Sonata for Piano, op. 31 no. 3, in E♭
       major


334    "Die Jahreszeiten"   (see "The Seasons")
       Louis Spohr.   Symphony No. 9 in B minor, op. 143


335    "Jena Symphony"
       Friedrich Witt.   Symphony in C major

        This work had been attributed to Beethoven but it has
been proven that this was not so.   In 1900 Fritz Stein discovered what he thought was an unknown early symphony by
Beethoven.   His source was a set of old manuscript parts
in the archives of Akademisches Konzert in the university
town of Jena.   Beethoven's name appeared on the second
violin part ("Par Louis van Beethoven").   Subsequently Stein
edited a score of the work, which was published under
Beethoven's name by Breitkopf und Härtel.   However, critical opinion on the authenticity of the symphony had been divided.   In an article in the Music Review of 1957 [p. 109],
H. C. Robbins Landon has a different story.   He found an
entry in the Gottweig Catalogue which is identical to the
Jena Symphony and was composed by Friedrich Witt.   It
seems that the Jena parts were originally acquired as by

Witt and later the title page was lost and someone added
Beethoven's name.   Landon goes on to say that when Stein
went into the details more fully and examined the watermarks on the paper of Jena source he said, "I could find
paper of this kind only in one other work among the music
of the archives, an A major symphony by Friedrich Witt,
all the wind parts of which contain the same watermarks.
        Secondly, the Jena Symphony had an old catalogue
number 24 while the A major symphony by Witt was 26.
Thirdly (and with this the puzzle was solved) the first violin
part of the Jena manuscript had the following initials in the
lower hand corner:  "(P. F. W.). "  Obviously Jena had purchased a series of Witt symphonies including this work.


336   "Jeunehomme"
      Mozart.   Concerto for Piano in E♭ major   (K.  271)

        Mozart wrote this concerto in January 1777 and in a
letter ten months later refers to it as the one for the
"Jenome. "  He meant Mlle. Jeunchomme, a celebrated
French pianist who, in one of her tours, had evidently
visited Salzburg, and for whom Mozart had written the concerto.   One would like to know more about Mlle. Jeunehomme, but unfortunately she remains a legendary figure.


337   "Jig Fugue"
      J. S. Bach.   Fugue for Organ in G major   (BWV 577)

        The Fugue in G major, originally composed for a two-
manual and pedal harpsichord, is written in a 12/8 sprightly
"jig-like" rhythm.   Spitta feels that Bach was greatly influenced by Buxtehude in the writing of this composition, but
Harvey Grace [Organ Works of Bach, p. 38] says that actually the "Jig Fugue" owes more to the old Italian string
composers than to Buxtehude.


338   "The Joke"
      Haydn.   Quartet, op. 33 no. 2, in E♭ major   (Hob.
      III,  38)

        The "joke" of this one, earning the special title within
the general nickname for the Op. 33 quartets--"Gli Scherzi"
("the joke")--is the amusing foolishness in the Finale.   After
a solemn Adagio episode, the eight measures of the main

theme are repeated in a strange manner.    Each phrase of
two bars is followed by a rest of two measures.    When the
entire theme is played, Haydn doubles the rest and starts
all over again with the first measures of the melody.    This
leaves the listener puzzled and amused.
        Here is another story about the nickname reflecting
Haydn's bent for mischievous fun.    In the finale, a rondo,
he tried to prove that women are always involved in gossip
while listening to music.    To catch them he put in a short
Adagio at the close of the movement after which he repeated
the principal theme, inserting a two-bar rest after each
phrase.    Then he included a four-bar rest before repeating
the opening phrase of the theme.    These pauses were intended to reveal the gossiping women [from Milton Cross
and David Ewen, Encyclopedia of the Great Composers, v.
1, p. 28].


339    "The Joyous Peasant"  (see "Songs Without Words")
       Mendelssohn.    Piece for Piano, op. 102 no. 5, in A
       major


340    "Jullien"
       G. F. Bristow.    Symphony in D minor

       The subtitle was as a compliment to Louis Antoine
Jullien, a French conductor and composer who visited the
United States in 1853-54 and while here conducted this sym-
phony on one of his programs.


341    "Jungfernquartette"  (see "Russian Quartets")
       Haydn.    Quartets, op. 33  (Hob. III, 37-42)


342    "Jupiter"
       Mozart.    Symphony in C major  (K. 551)

       No one knows for certain who first nicknamed this
symphony more than a century ago, but it has been sus-
pected that J. B. Cramer, pianist and teacher, was responsible for it.    Although this symphony is the most classical
of the final group of three, there is nothing particularly
divine about it.    Mozart would have been the first to point
with amusement to the fact that there is nothing "Olympian"
in the little G major theme in the first movement, which

Eric Blom says he borrowed quite shamelessly from a comic
aria he had composed earlier, "Un Bacio di Mano" (K. 541),
of which the words are, "You are a little dense, my dear
Pompeo, go and study the ways of the world. "
        Philip Hale, the famous music critic, said of the
symphony, "There is nothing in the music that reminds one
of Jupiter.   The music is not of an Olympian mood.   It is
undoubtedly intensely human in its loveliness and gaity. "


343   "Kaffee-Cantate"   (see "Coffee Cantata")
      J. S. Bach.   Cantata, op. 211   (BWV 211)


344   "Der Kaffeeklatsch   (see "Gossips at the Coffee Table")
      Haydn.   No. 18 of Set of Pieces for Musical Clocks
      (Hob. XIX, 6)


345   "Das kecke Beserl"   (see "The Saucy Maid")
      Bruckner.   Symphony No. 1 in C minor


346   "Kegelstatt Trio"   (see "Skittle Ground Trio")
      Mozart.   Trio for Piano, Clarinet and Viola   (K. 498)


347   "Keltic"
      MacDowell.   Sonata for Piano No. 4, op. 59, in E
        minor

        The Celtic (or, Keltic) legend about the beautiful Deir-
dre, daughter of the harper King Conchobar, inspired Mac-
Dowell to subtitle the piano sonata "Keltic. "   Above the
dedication to Edward Grieg, MacDowell put the following
quatrain: "Who minds now Keltic days of Yore/ Dark Druid
rhymes that thrall/ Deirdre's Song and wizard lore/ of
Great Cuchulin's fall. "


348   "Kettledrum Mass" [Paukenmesse]
      Haydn.   Mass in C major (Hob. XXII, 9)

        During the summer of 1796, while Haydn was working
on this mass, Napoleon's armies were across the Styrian
border pressing towards Leoben.   Haydn was greatly affected
by this and wrote "Missa in tempore belli" ("Mass in

Wartime") at the top of the score.

There is no doubt that the use of the kettledrums and trumpets in the Agnus Dei and the fanfare of wind instruments at the beginning of the Dona Nobis Pacem emphasize the war atmosphere. The nickname "Kettledrum" is derived from the drumroll in the Agnus Dei.

349 "King of Prussia"
Mozart. Three String Quartets: in D major (K. 575); in B♭ major (K. 589); and F major (K. 590)

These three quartets, which are Mozart's last string quartets, were written at the request of the King of Prussia. They were written with an intended dedication to him but somehow the first edition was published without the dedication. The King was a cellist and in deference to him Mozart wrote a prominent cello part in each of the quartets and they have always been known as the "King of Prussia quartets."

350 "Eine kleine Nachtmusik" (see "A little Night Music")
Mozart. Serenade for Strings in G major (K. 525)

351 "Kleine Orgel-Messe" (see "Little Organ Mass")
Haydn. Missa St. Joannes de Deo, in B♭ major (Hob. XXII, 7)

352 "Kreutzer Sonata"
Beethoven. Sonata for Violin and Piano, no. 9, op. 47 in A major

The young mulatto violinist, Bridgetower, came to Vienna from England in early 1803 and made a great impression on Beethoven. The composer wrote this A major Sonata for him, for a performance at a morning concert at the Augarten (probable date, May 24). The sonata was not quite ready when the date for performance arrived and it was played from the manuscript. According to Bridgetower's memorandum on the copy of the score, Beethoven performed the slow movement with such "chaste expression" that it was encored.

Unfortunately, Beethoven and Bridgetower had a bitter quarrel, apparently over a girl, before the sonata was published, and Beethoven changed the dedication to the prominent Parisian violinist, Rudolph Kreutzer. Although the piece has always been known by its popular name "Kreutzer Sonata" it is said that Kreutzer never performed the sonata in public.

Another interesting thing about the sonata is that when the great Tolstoy heard the work ninety years after it was published, he was so impressed with it that he named his novel "Kreutzer Sonata. "


353  "Kronungs-Konzert"  (see "Coronation Concerto")
     Mozart.   Concerto for Piano in D major   (K. 537)


354  "Kronungs-Messe"  (see "Coronation Mass")
     Mozart.   Mass in C major   (K. 317)


355  "Kulavy"
     Chopin.   Mazurka for Piano in G major   (Brown 17)

This mazurka has been nicknamed because of the style of the dance, "Kulavy Lame. " It was improvised by Chopin during dance entertainments at the home of Dr. Samuel Linde, the Rector of the Warsaw Lyceum. It was written down by friends of Chopin.


356  "Kurfürsten Sonatas"
     Beethoven.   Three Sonatas for Piano in E♭ major, F
        minor and D major   (WoO 47)

These were composed by Beethoven for the Kurfürst (Elector) of Cologne, Archbishop Maximilian Frederick, when he was said to be 11 but was actually 13.


357  "Ländliche Hochzeit"  (see "Rustic Wedding")
     Carl Goldmark.   Symphony in E♭ major, op. 26


358  "Lamentatione"
     Haydn.   Symphony No. 26 in D minor   (Hob. I, 26)

H. C. Robbins Landon in his book, The Symphonies of Joseph Haydn, says that the title "Christmas Symphony" under which this symphony is sometimes known is completely

erroneous.  He feels very definitely that the work was composed for the Easter Week and not for the Nativity.
    Landon has the following to say, which makes the
subtitle "Lamentatione" the correct one.  "The title of the
oldest MS, that in the abbey at Herzogenburg, is 'Passio
et Lamentis,' and it was from the remarks penned over the
second violin part in this source that the present writer
came to the conclusion that the first and second movements
illustrate some drama played during the Holy Week.  Hap-
pily it has been possible to discover the origin of the entire Symphony through several rare prints, copies of which
are found in various Monasteries and churches in Austria"
[p. 286].


359  "Il Lamento e la Consolazione"
     Chopin.  Nocturnes for Piano, op. 32  (Brown 106)


360  "Largo Quartet"
     Haydn.  Quartet, op. 76 no. 5, in D major  (Hob.
       III, 79)

    The largo of this quartet attains such a plane of elo-
quence that the entire work has been designated as the
"Largo Quartet. "


361  "The Lark"
     Haydn.  String Quartet, op. 64 no. 5, in D major
       (Hob. III, 67)

    The lovely first movement of this quartet has given it
the popular name of "The Lark. "  Geiringer, in his book,
Haydn:  A Creative Life in Music, says, "From the earth
bound accompaniment of the lower parts, the first violin
soars up to heavenly heights" [p. 286].


362  "The Last Musical Thought" (Der Letzte musikalische
       Gedanke)
     Beethoven.    Piece for Piano in B♭ major
       (WoO 60)

    This misleading title derives from the first separately
published edition of this piano piece.  The publisher,
Schlesinger in Berlin, in 1840 used the title, "Dernière

Pensée Musicale de Louis van Beethoven, " although the
piece was written on August 14, 1818, perhaps for Marie
Szymanowska.   It was first published as a supplement to
the Berlin Allgemeine Zeitung in 1824 and the following
year in the English journal Harmonicon with the title, "Im-
promptu Composed at the Dinner Table. "  Schlesinger's edition was copied by Hoffman in Prague, with the title, "Der
letzte musicalische Gedanke. "  The piece is found in the
Breitkopf und Härtel edition of Beethoven's works, Series
25 No. 38.


363   "The Last Musical Thought" [Der Letzte musikalische
        Gedanke]
        Beethoven.   Piece for Piano in C major (WoO
        62)

The last work which Beethoven began in November
1826, four months before his death, was a string quintet.
Although the autograph disappeared more than a century
ago, the composer-publisher Diabelli brought out a piano
transcription in C major of the introduction to the first
movement, with the title, "Ludwig van Beethovens letzte
musikalische Gedanke. "  This was contained in a collection, "Wiener Lieblingsstücke der neuesten Zeit für das
Pianoforte allein oder zu vier Händen" [favorite Viennese
pieces of today for piano alone or for four hands].
        It seems that this piano piece in C major is the
real "Last Musical Thought" and not the one in B♭ major
(previous entry).


364   "Laube-Sonate"   (see "Moonlight Sonata")
        Beethoven.   Sonata for Piano in C♯ minor, op. 27
        no. 2


365   "Laudon"
        Haydn.   Symphony No. 69 in C major   (Hob. I, 69)

Haydn suggested the nickname for this symphony for
two reasons.   First, as a compliment to the famous Austrian Field Marshall General Laudon, and secondly with the
hope that the well-known name would attract more sales.
        After Haydn arranged the symphony for the piano,
he wrote the following to his publisher Artaria (April 8,
1783) "I am sending you the Symphony [No. 69] which was

so full of mistakes that one ought to box the ears of the
fellow who wrote it.   The fourth and last movement of this
Symphony is not practicable for the clavier.   I don't think
it necessary to print it.   The word 'Laudon' will do more
towards selling the work than any ten finales. "

366   "Lebensstürme" ("Life's Tempest")
      Schubert.   Duet for Piano, op. 144 (D. 947)

      Einstein, in his book on Schubert, says the following
of this nickname:   "When we find a piano duet which Schubert wrote in his last years labeled 'Lebensstürme' by the
publisher (not by Schubert himself) the effect is much the
same as that of a bad illustration to a good poem, which
detracts from its subject and which obscures rather than
clarifies it" [p. 81].

367   "Leib Quartett"
      Beethoven.   String Quartet, op. 130, in B♭ major

      Beethoven himself called this his "Leib Quartett. "
This is a term of familiar endearment which the English
language lacks.   Many of the pages of this work represent
the most intimate emotional self-revelations that Beethoven
has left.

368   "Leitgebisches Quintet"
      Mozart.   Quintet for Horn and Strings in E♭ major
      (K. 407)

      Ignaz Leitgeb was a horn player from Salzburg who
settled in Vienna and for whom most of the horn music of
the period was written.   Mozart wrote the quintet in E♭
major for horn, violin, two violas and cello for him.   Einstein in his book, Mozart, His Character, His Work, says:
      "Like all the works written for this butt of Mo-
zart's jokes, it is to be taken half humorously.   One might
take it wholly so if it were not that the middle movement,
an Andante, is a deeply felt piece, a little love duet between horn and violin.   The first and the last movement
make sport of the limitations of the solo instrument--listen
especially to the humorous fanfare-motive in the Rondo-
Finale" [p. 194].

369   "Leningrad"
      Shostakovich.   Symphony No. 7

The Seventh Symphony of Shostakovich is really a glorification of the heroic city of Leningrad.   The first movement was completed in Leningrad on September 3, 1941,
the second on September 17, 1941, the third on September
29, 1941 and the last movement in Kuibishev on December
27, 1941.
      Shostakovich says the following about this work:
"My Seventh Symphony is inspired by the great events of
our patriotic war, but it is not battle music.   The first
movement is dedicated to the struggle, and the fourth to
victory....   No more noble mission can be conceived than
that which spurs us on to fight against the dark forces of
Hitlerism.   That is why the roar of the cannon does not
keep the Muses of our people from lifting their voices. "


370   "Lenore"
      Joachim Raff.   Symphony No. 5 in E major, op. 177


371   "Letter A (etc.)"
      Haydn.   Nine Symphonies with Letters

In England during the 19th century a number of Haydn's
symphonies were identified by their letters in the old catalogue of the Royal Philharmonic Society, thus:   A. Symphony
No. 71 B♭ major; D. Symphony No. 45 F♯ minor ("Farewell"); E. Symphony No. 44 E minor ("Funeral"); L. Symphony No. 47 G major; Q. Symphony No. 92 G major ("Oxford"); R. Symphony No. 90 C major; T. Symphony No. 91
E♭ major; V. Symphony No. 88 G major; and W. Symphony
No. 89 F major.


372   "Der letzte musikalische Gedanke"   (see "Last Musical
         Thought")
      Beethoven.   Pieces for Piano in B♭ major and C ma-
         jor   (WoO 60 and 62)


373   "Life's Tempest"   (see "Lebensstürme")
      Schubert.   Duet for Piano, op. 144   (D. 947)

374    "Lincoln"
D. G. Mason.    Symphony No. 3

In his Third Symphony, Daniel Gregory Mason depicts
various periods of Lincoln's life.    The first movement describes Lincoln's early manhood and a popular song of the
1860's, "Quaboag," is used prominently.    The second movement is patterned after a spiritual to portray the Negro's
tenderness for Lincoln.    The amusing scherzo is typical of
Lincoln's broad sense of humor, and the symphony ends
with a lament for the assassinated president.


375    "Linz"
Mozart.    Symphony in C major    (K. 425)

In a letter Mozart wrote to his father from Linz,
dated October 31, 1783, he tells him that he had arrived
there the day before and after being entertained by Count
Thun, had been asked for a symphony for a concert to be
held on November 4th.    Unfortunately, he had neglected to
bring one and he was "up to his neck" composing a new
one.
        It is almost unbelievable to comprehend a symphony
being composed, copied, rehearsed and performed in a
period of four days, but this was the case with the wonderful C major Symphony, the so-called "Linz. "


376    "Listy Duverné"    (see "Intimate Pages")
Leoš Janáček.    String Quartet No. 2


377    "The Little"
J. S. Bach.    Fugue in G minor for Organ    (BWV 578)

The Fugue in G minor was nicknamed "The Little" by
the organists in order to distinguish it from the more im-
posing Fantasy and Fugue in the same key.    Bach wrote
this during the years 1708 to 1717 when he was court organist to the Duke of Weimar.    It is one of his most popular organ works and understandably so.


378    "The Little"
Schubert.    Symphony No. 6 in C major    (D. 589)

The symphony was written between October 1817 and February 1818. The reason for it being nicknamed "The Little" was to distinguish it from the more familiar and longer Seventh Symphony in the same key. Schubert was originally supposed to have composed this symphony for the amateur orchestra that grew out of the string quartet which used to play at his father's school.

379   "The Little Jew"
      Chopin.   Mazurka in A minor, op. 17 no. 4   (Brown
      7)

Brown reports that this may be the work referred to by Chopin in the little mock newspaper ("The Szafarnian Courier," September 3, 1824) which he and his sister Emilia devised for family reading and amusement in the summer of 1824 from Szafarnia. He reported "Mr. Pichon [an anagram of Chopin] played 'The Little Jew'." This suggestion was first put forward tentatively by Marcel Antoine Szulc (1873), but it has been taken up by subsequent biographers as if it were an established fact. Szafarnia was part of the estate of the friend of the Chopin family, Dominik Dzyewanour Dzyewanowski.

380   "A Little Night Music" (Eine Kleine Nachtmusik)
      Mozart.   Serenade for Strings in G major   (K. 525)

The serenades were usually written for a small group of wind players at the request of some important person and were performed in the garden for an evening party. This Serenade in G major, which Mozart nicknamed, "Eine Kleine Nachtmusik," is an exception. Mozart wrote it for strings and we do not know for certain what the occasion was. It might have been for a performance in Vienna.
      Einstein, in his book Mozart, His Character, His Work, feels that Mozart probably wrote the work for himself to satisfy an inner need, perhaps even as a counterpart to the "Musical Joke" which he had recently composed and which bothered his sensitive musical soul. Whatever the reason might have been, the charming festive feeling of the music has made it one of the most popular of Mozart's instrumental works.

381   "Little Organ Mass"
      Haydn.   Missa St. Joannes de Deo in B♭ major
      (Hob. XXII, 7)

The Missa St. Joannes de Deo, nicknamed "Little Organ Mass," is written for four voices, two violins, and organ solo.   In the Benedictus the organ part actually competes with the solo soprano.   It is interesting to see that in Haydn's original manuscript of the mass, the notes of the bass and the organ part were written about twice as large as the notes of the other part.   This was probably done to indicate that the organist intended to play from the full score; perhaps it was for Haydn himself.

382   "Little Russian"
      Tchaikovsky.   Symphony No. 2, op. 17, in C minor

While Tchaikovsky was on a visit to St. Petersburg about Easter 1868, he came in contact with a group of young musicians who were working for the cause of nationality in art.   It was at this time that he wrote his Second Symphony, which got its nickname from Nicholas Kaskin, a Moscow art critic and teacher.
      The symphony is based upon little Russian folk tunes.   Particularly effective are the use of "Down by Mother Volga" in the first movement and "The Crane" in the third one.

383   "A Little Symphony"
      Carl Eppert.   Symphony No. 2, op. 65

The composer says that he subtitled his Symphony No. 2 so because it is scored for a Mozart-type orchestra, plus harp.

384   "Little Trumpet Piece"
      Mendelssohn.   Scherzo for Piano in E minor

Mendelssohn called this scherzo his "Little Trumpet Piece."   The beginning of the scherzo has a trumpet-like theme which reappears several times during the short composition.

385   "Liturgique"
      Honegger.   Symphony No. 3

Honegger says, about his Symphony No. 3, "Each of
the three sections endeavors to express an idea, a thought
which I should presume to call philosophical, but which is
my own personal feeling.   I have therefore called upon
liturgical subtitles and given the work the name of "Liturgical Symphony. "
      Nicolas Slonimsky, in his Music since 1900, goes
further to explain the subtitles of the movements.   "The
three movements subtitled 'Dies Irae' (in apocalyptically
strident chromatics, devoid of any thematic illusion to the
traditional chant, with giant intervallic strides suggesting
an atonal Doomsday), 'De Profundis Clamavi' (in dejected
low tunes, torturously and tortuously rising to shrill heights,
of polytonal anxiety), and 'Dona Nobis Pacem' (an imploring
prayer for peace, against the rumble of distant drums of
war, with a diatonic hopefulness dashed again and again by
chromatic bursts of despair).... " [p. 577].


386   "Lobgesang"   (see "Hymn of Praise")
      Mendelssohn.   Symphony No. 2 in B♭ major for Or-
         chestra and Voices


387   "Lodron"
      Mozart.   Concerto for Three Pianos No. 7 in F major
         (K. 242)

Mozart wrote his Concerto for Three Pianos in February 1776 and it is in his father's dedication, written in
Italian, that the reason for the popular title "Lodron" is
given:   "To the incomparable merit of Her excellency,
Signorina Contessa Lodron, born Contessa d'Arco, and her
daughters, the Signorine Contesse Aloysia and Josepha. "
      The three ladies were apparently not all "incompar-
able" because one of the parts is much simpler than the
other two; as a matter of fact Mozart made an alternate
arrangement of the concerto for two pianos, which is actually an improvement on the three-piano one.


388   "London"
      Haydn.   Symphonies 93-104   (Hob. I, 93-104)

These last 12 symphonies, numbers 93 through 104,
were written for the London violinist and impresario, Salomon, and have always been known as either the "London"
or "Salomon" Symphonies.   The character of the works was
to a great extent the result of the circumstances under
which they were written.   According to H. C. Robbins Landon [The Symphonies, p. 552] Haydn wrote "a good deal
[that] must be altered to suit the English taste. "


389    "London Symphony"
       Haydn.   Symphony No. 104 in D major   (Hob. I, 104)

       The last of the 12 "London Symphonies, " the D major,
No. 104, is everywhere known as the "London Symphony. "
Actually no one knows why this particular one has been
singled out for the nickname, as any one of the 12 is right-
fully eligible.


390    "A London Symphony"
       Vaughan Williams.   Symphony No. 2

       This symphony is a musical picture of the city of Lon-
don.   The conductor, Albert Coates, an intimate friend of
the composer, describes the work in the following manner:
"I.  London sleeps.   The Thames flows serenely through the
city.   The city awakens.   We get different glimpses of the
city--its varied character--its good humor--its activity.
II.  Portrait of the region known as Bloomsbury.   It is dusk
--damp and foggy twilight.   There is poverty everywhere-
poverty and tragedy.   An old musician outside a pub plays
'Sweet Lavender. '  The gloom deepens.   The movement ends
with the musician still playing his sad tune.
       "III. Sitting late one Saturday evening at the Temple
Embankment.   On one side of the river are the slums; on
the other, the stately majesty of the Houses of Parliament.
The Thames River flows serenely.   IV.  A picture of the
crueler side of the city; the unemployed; the unfortunate.
The music ends as it began--with the Thames flowing
silently, serenely. "


391    "The London Trios" [Die Londoner Trios]
       Haydn.   Four Trios for two Flutes and Violoncello
       (Hob. IV, 1-4) No. 1 in C major; No. 2 in G major;
       No. 3 in G major; and No. 4 in G major

In an edition of these Trios published in 1931 by
Nagels Verlag, Hannover, there is the following note by the
editor, Leo Balet:

"According to the signed and dated original manu-
scripts, Joseph Haydn composed Trios I, II, and III, in
London in 1794.  He was sixty years old at that time.
Trio IV, which has been preserved for us from this period
only in a transcript, probably belongs to the same group.
The original scores are in the Prussian State Library.
Trios I, II, and III, have already appeared in imperfect edi-
tions.  Trio II appears here for the first time in print.... "


392  "Loss"
     Chopin.   Prelude, op. 28 no. 13, in F♯ major
     (Brown 107, no. 13)

     Each of Chopin's Op. 28 preludes was given a subtitle
by Hans von Bülow.  Of this one he writes, "Chopin grieves;
he cannot see his loved one and holds her as lost forever.
He is convinced that she loves him no longer and his woe
finds expression in music; every note in the left hand pro-
claims it, the same tones are repeated over and over per-
sistently.  In the passage in D sharp minor the memory of
the past is heard; now in the upper voice, now in the lower.
In the last two measures before the tempo primo one fairly
hears his groans and stifled sighs over his loss, while in
the tempo primo itself resignation wins the upper hand"
[Musician, xvi (1911)].


303  "Lost Happiness"  (see "Songs Without Words")
     Mendelssohn.  Piece for Piano, op. 38 no. 2, in C
     minor


394  "Lost Illusion"  (see "Songs Without Words")
     Mendelssohn.  Piece for Piano, op. 67 no. 1, in F
     minor


395  "The Lover"
     Scarlatti.  Sonata for Piano  (L. 108, K. 213)


396  "Lucio Silla"
     J. C. Bach.   Sinfonia in B♭ major, op. 18 no. 2

It was this sinfonia which prefaced Johann Christian Bach's opera, <u>Lucio Silla</u>. He wrote it for the opera house in Mannheim and it was based on a libretto by Giovanna da Campera about the Roman general Lucius Silla. Hence the subtitle.

397  "Lyric"
     Bruckner.  Symphony No. 7 in E major

This symphony is so called because it is inspired by the spirit of song. It is warm, radiant lyric and no other subtitle would be more fitting.

398  "Madrigalesco"
     Vivaldi.  Concerto for Strings and Harpsichord in D
        minor  (F. XI, 10)

399  "A Maggot"
     T. A. Arne.  Organ Concerto No. 3 (2d movt, "Con
        Spirito")

400  "Maiden Quartets" [Jungfernquartette]  (see "Russian
        Quartets")
     Haydn.  Quartets, op. 33  (Hob. III, 37-42)

401  "March for the Prince of Wales"
     Haydn.  March in E♭ for Small Orchestra  (Hob. VIII,
        3)

This march, which Haydn wrote for the Prince of Wales, was "discovered" and first printed in score form by Karl Haas. It is interesting to see that even though it is a work on a small scale, it is unmistakably the work of a master.

402  "Marche Militaire"
     Schubert.  March, op. 51 no. 3, in D major for Piano
        Solo (orig. Piano Four hands)  (D. 733, No. 1)

On August 7, 1826, three Schubert marches, Op. 51, composed for piano four hands, were published by Diabelli.

Of the set of three, D major, C major and E♭ major, the
D major one has been arranged for various combinations
and has received worldwide popularity.   In this arrangement
for piano solo it has been extremely successful and everyone knows it by its nickname.

403   "Maria Theresia"
      Haydn.   Symphony No. 48 in C major   (Hob. I, 48)

      In 1773 the Empress Maria Theresa visited Esterháza
and there was much festivity.    Special music was performed
and Haydn wrote this symphony for the occasion.    To give
it a festive and brilliant air, Haydn added trumpets and
drums to the more standard orchestration of oboes, horns
and strings that he had used in his other symphonies.
      The Wiener Diarium gave detailed accounts of the
festivities; pertinent to the symphony it said, "Then the
Empress was taken to the Chinese pavilion, whose mirror-
covered walls reflected countless lampions and chandeliers
flooding the room with light.    On a platform sat the princely
orchestra in gala uniform and played under Haydn's direction his new Symphony 'Maria Theresia'. " The Empress was
so pleased with the music that she presented Haydn with a
valuable golden snuffbox filled with ducats.

404   "Mariazellermesse"
      Haydn.   Mass in C major (Missa Cellensis)   (Hob.
      XXII, 8)

      Mariazell, 60 miles from Vienna, is the most famous
place of pilgrimage in Austria.    A Benedictine monastery is
located there and it is supposed that Anton Liebe von
Kreutzner, a recently ennobled government official, commissioned this Mass as a votive offering to the Monastery.

405   "Mass in Wartime"   (see "Kettledrum Mass")
      Haydn.   Mass in C major (Missa in Tempore Belli)
      (Hob. XXII, 9)

406   "Le Matin, le Midi, et le Soir" [Morning, Midday, and
      Evening]
      Haydn.   Trilogy of symphonies:   No. 6 Le Matin in
      D major; No. 7 Le Midi in C major; No. 8 Le Soir
      in G major (Hob. I, 6, 7, & 8)

Haydn was engaged as assistant Capellmeister to the
Court of Prince Anton Esterházy in May 1761. The first
symphonies which he composed for his new patron appear to
have been a trilogy named after the times of the day. According to Haydn's biographer, Dies, the idea for this was
suggested to Haydn by the prince.

407 "La Matinée"
J. L. Dussek. Sonata for Piano, op. 25 no. 2

408 "May Breezes" (see "Songs Without Words")
Mendelssohn. Piece for Piano, op. 62 no. 1, in G
major

409 "May First"
Shostakovich. Symphony No. 3, op. 20, for Chorus
and Orchestra

The Third Symphony bears the inscription "May First"
and was written to commemorate the annual May Day Celebration in the Soviet Union. The motivation of the Symphony
is indicated in the words sung by the chorus at its conclusion:
"Today on this gleaming May festival let our songs
resound.... Before in the gloomy years we went timidly
and afraid.... When the Winter still was gray, and shoot-
ing still was heard on the field of war, an army of workers
and peasants stormed the palace of the Tsar. Daringly the
step was taken, onward our path leads us.... Mighty and
ever stronger The Great Plan goes forward to become a
fact. Immense new works spring from the new seed. Coal,
grain, steel, that is a new radiance.... The land belongs
to the workers, the age is theirs.... Every May Day is a
step nearer to our socialistic goal. Solemnly through the
cities millions of us surge."
The symphony is in one movement with choral ending, although when the American premiere of the work was
given by Stokowski and the Philadelphia Orchestra in December 1932, it was presented without chorus. The actual
premiere of the symphony was in Leningrad, November 6,
1930.

410    "Meditation"    (see "Songs Without Words")
       Mendelssohn.    Piece for Piano, op. 67 no. 1, in E♭
       major


411    "Meistersinger"
       Brahms.    Sonata for Violin and Piano, op. 100, in A
       major

       When the sonata first appeared there was a chance
similarity noticed between the first three notes of the principal theme of the first movement and those of Walter's
Preislied in Wagner's opera, Die Meistersinger.    Immediately it was labeled "Meistersinger. "
       It is also known by the nickname "Thun. "  Brahms
spent a happy summer on the lake of Thun in 1886, and it
was there that the sonata was composed.    The following poem, written by his friend, Widmann, describes the setting.
"Dort wo die Aare sanft dem See entgleitet/ Zur kleinen
Stadt hinab, die sie bespült/ Und Schatten mancher gute
Baum verbreitet/ Hatt' ich mich tief ins hohe Gras gewühlt/
Und schlief und träumt' am hellen Sommertag/ So köstlich,
wie ich kaum es künden mag" [There where the Aar glides
softly from the lake down to the little town which it washes,
and many a noble tree spreads its shadow, I rolled deep in
the long grass and slept, and dreamed through the bright
summer day, dreams so delicious that I could hardly describe them].


412    "Melk"
       Haydn.   Concerto for Violin and Orchestra in A major
       (Hob. VIIa, 3)

       This concerto has been nicknamed "Melk" because the
only known copy in existence is in the monastery in Melk
(Lower Austria).   It was discovered by the Haydn Society
and the score was published by the Haydn Mozart Presse,
Salzburg, in 1952, edited by Anton Heiller and H. C. Robbins Landon.   There is a recording of this work made by
the Haydn Society, the first known performance since Haydn's
lifetime.


413    "Mercury" [Le Merkur]
       Haydn.   Symphony No. 43 in E♭ major (Hob. I, 43)

This symphony seems to date from the year 1772.
The autograph of the work has been lost but a critical text
was supplied by comparing old manuscript parts from the
Benedictine cloisters of Göttweig and Kremsmünster in
Austria, as well as MSS. in the Prince Oettinger Waller-
stein collection in Schloss Harburg, Bavaria. The work
first appeared in the Breitkopf catalogue of the year 1772
and immediately became very popular. The reason for the
subtitle is not entirely clear but appears to refer to the
very effective outer movement with its quick moving 16th
notes.


414   "Le Midi"  (see "Le Matin, Le Midi et Le Soir")
      Haydn.  Symphony No. 7 in C major  (Hob. I, 7)


415   "Midi"  (see "Twelve o'clock")
      John Field.  Rondo for Piano in E major  (Hopkinson
      13 K.)


416   "Militaire" [Military]
      Chopin.  Polonaise for Piano, op. 40 no. 1, in A
      major  (Brown 120)

    The polonaise is a stately dance of Polish origin.
Chopin animated the dry form of the old polonaise with
great spirit and martial rhythm. This is particularly true
in the popular so-called "Military Polonaise." It is a
noisy piece with powerful rhythm and exemplifies military
assertiveness in all its glory.


417   "Military"
      Haydn.  Symphony No. 100 in G major  (Hob. I, 100)

    It seems that to 18th-century ears drums, cymbals and
triangles suggested the Turks, and the Turks personified
war. Therefore, any use of these percussion instruments
was immediately associated with war. Since Haydn used
these instruments and particularly wrote a military trumpet
call in the coda of the Allegretto movement of this symphony, it was immediately nicknamed "Military."

418    "Minute Waltz" (also, "Dog Waltz")
       Chopin.   Waltz for Piano, op. 64 no. 1, in D major
       (Brown 164, no. 1)

There have been two nicknames given to this famous
waltz, "Minute Waltz" and "Dog Waltz. "  "Minute Waltz"
is not really a very exact nickname because it actually takes
one and a half minutes to perform the piece well.   However, the name has lent itself to amusing stories.   A well
known one is of the two pianists attending a concert in
Carnegie Hall where it was played; one of them commented
to the other how badly it had been played in that it took
much longer than one minute adding, "You know, this was
the dullest quarter of an hour I have ever spent. "
       The origin of the other nickname, "Dog Waltz, " is
attributed to George Sand.   It was at her suggestion that
Chopin improvized this waltz with the revolving right hand
melody imitating her dog chasing his own tail.


419    "The Miracle"
       Haydn.   Symphony No. 102 in D major   (Hob. I, 102)

According to Robbins Landon [The Symphonies of Joseph
Haydn, p. 534], it has always been thought that the Symphony No. 96 was the so called "Miracle. "   But this was
not so.   He cites a review in the London Morning Chronicle
of February 3, 1794, after the first performance of Symphony No. 102, in which the following incident was reported:
       "When Haydn appeared in the orchestra and seated
himself at the pianoforte to conduct a symphony personally
the curious audience in the parterre left their seats and
pressed forward to the orchestra with a view to seeing
Haydn better at close range.   The seats in the middle of
the parterre were therefore empty and no sooner were they
empty but a great chandelier plunged down, smashed and
threw the numerous company into great confusion.   As soon
as the first moment of shock was over, and those who had
pressed forward realized the danger which they had so
luckily escaped and could find words to express the same,
many persons showed their state of mind by shouting loudly,
"Miracle, Miracle. "


420    "Missa Cellensis" (see "Cantata Mass")
       Haydn.   Saint Cecilia Mass in C major   (Hob. XXII, 5)

421   "Missa in Angustiis"  (see "Nelson Mass")
      Haydn.   Mass in D minor   (Hob. XXII, 11)


422   "Missa in tempore belli"  (see "Kettledrum Mass")
      Haydn.   Mass in C major   (Hob. XXII, 9)


423   "Missa Solemnis"
      Beethoven.   Mass in D major, op. 123

      "Missa Solemnis" is a title used by various composers
for a mass of a particularly elaborate festive kind, but it
is now associated mainly with Beethoven's Mass in D major.
      It was known in 1818 that the Archduke Rudolph was
to be appointed Archbishop of Olmütz and in that year
Beethoven began to compose this Mass in D, subtitled "Missa Solemnis," with the intention of having it performed at
the ceremony of installation.   When the ceremony took place
in March 1820, the composition had proceeded no further
than the Credo.   In 1821, Beethoven opened dealings with
the publisher, Simrock, as if the mass were completed,
but two more years passed before he finished revising it.
The first performance took place in Vienna on May 7, 1824.


424   "Mit dem Paukenschlag"  (see "Surprise Symphony")
      Haydn.   Symphony No. 94, in G major   (Hob. I, 94)


425   "Moby Dick"
      Peter Mennin.   Concertato for Orchestra

      The composer has provided [in the Philadelphia Orches-
tra Program Notes, 1972] the following background of the
subtitle:  "Late in 1951 a libretto based on the Melville novel
Moby Dick was submitted to me to consider as material for
an opera.   Reading the libretto in rough sketch made me de-
cide to compose the Concertato and subtitle it 'Moby Dick. '
This, then is a dramatic work for orchestra motivated by
the Melville novel seeking to depict the emotional impact of
the work as a whole rather than musically describing iso-
lated movements. "


426   "Mondschein-Sonate"  (see "Moonlight Sonata")
      Beethoven.   Sonata for Piano in C♯ minor, op. 27 no.
      2

427   "Moonlight Sonata" [Mondschein-Sonate]
      Beethoven.   Sonata for Piano in C# minor, op. 27 no.
      2

      Many stories have been written about the origin of the
nickname "Moonlight Sonata." The following two are well
known.   (1) It is said to owe its origin to Rellstab, the
critic, who compared the first movement to a boat wander-
ing by moonlight on the Lake of Lucerne.   The only trouble
with this story is that Beethoven never visited the lake.
      (2) In H. E. Krehbiel's book, The Pianoforte and
Its Music [pp. 163-4], there is the following:   "The Sonata
in C# minor has asked many a tear from gentle souls who
were taught to hear in its first movement a lament for un-
requited love and reflected that it was dedicated to the
Countess Giulietta Guicciardi, for whom Beethoven assuredly
had a tender feeling.   Moonlight and the plaint of an unhappy lover.   How affecting but Beethoven did not compose
this Sonata for the Countess, though he inscribed it to her.
He had given her a Rondo, and wishing to dedicate it to
another pupil, he asked for its return and in exchange sent
the Sonata.   Moreover, it appears from evidence scarcely
to be gainsaid that Beethoven never intended the C# minor
Sonata as a musical expression of love, unhappy or otherwise." According to Thayer, Life of Beethoven [p. 297],
Beethoven had been asked to arrange the first movement of
this sonata to accompany the text of an insignificant poem,
"Die Beterin," by Johann Gottfried Seume,  and had indeed
promised to do so, but never did anything about it.


428   "Morning Song" (see "Songs Without Words")
      Mendelssohn.   Piece for Piano, op. 62 no. 4, in G
      major


429   "Mourning Symphony" (see "Trauer-Symphonie")
      Haydn.   Symphony No. 44 in E minor   (Hob. I, 44)


430   "Mozartiana"
      Tchaikovsky.   Suite No. 4 for Orchestra in G major

      In the Suite No. 4 Tchaikovsky borrowed some of Mo-
zart's themes from smaller, less known works and arranged
them for orchestra.   The composer, in the Preface to the
score, explains his reason for doing this as his desire to

bring these gems of musical literature to the attention of
the public.


431   "Murmures de la Seine"
      Chopin.   Nocturnes for Piano, op. 9   (Brown 54)


432   "Music in London"
      William Boyce.   Symphony No. 1 in B♭ major

      About 1760 Boyce published a set of eight symphonies.
The first one has always been known as "Music in London. "
It was originally an overture which Boyce had composed as
a royal New Year's Ode of 1756.   All three movements depict life in London, the first lively, the second slow and
sad and the third a boisterous jig.


433   "La musica notturna delle strade di Madrid"   (see
         "Night Music of the Streets of Madrid")
      Luigi Boccherini.   Quintet for two Violins, Viola and
         Two Cellos in C major, op. 30 no. 6   (Gérard 324)


434   "A Musical Joke" [Ein Musikalischer Spass]
      Mozart.   Divertimento in F major for Strings and
         Horn   (K. 522)

      Mozart was an inveterate joker but it is in that diverti-
mento that he uses this characteristic to distort music.   It
is the would-be composer that Mozart is poking fun at;
hence the nickname.
      The piece is full of wrong harmonies; chords are
wrongly distributed, the opening theme is choppy and ends
a bar too soon and trills are on wrong notes.   In the midst
of all this chaos, a few bars of ripply Mozartian music are
heard only to have a sudden jar of the horns, which does
not at all blend with the strings.   The final gesture is a
cadenza which seems to ridicule cadenzas and the presto
ends with harmonic confusion.


435   "Ein Musikalischer Spass"   (see "A Musical Joke")
      Mozart.   Divertimento in F major for Strings and
         Horns   (K. 522)

436   "Nacht Musique"  (see "Night Music")
      Mozart.  Serenade No. 12 in C minor  (K. 388)


437   Der Nachtwächter  (see "Witches Minuet")
      Haydn.  Minuet, of String Quartet, op. 76 no. 2, in
      D minor  (Hob. III, 76)


438   "Name-Day" [Namensfeier]
      Beethoven.  Overture, op. 115, in C major

      This overture was originally intended to be performed
on the Name-Day Festival of Emperor Franz, October 4,
1814.   Beethoven had written on the original manuscript
"Overture by L. v. Beethoven on the first of Wine Month,
1814, Evening, to the Name Day of our Emperor. " Com-
plications arose and although the overture was not performed on the date that Beethoven had intended, it had always been known as the "Name-Day" Overture.


439   "Namensfeier"  (see "Name-Day")
      Beethoven.  Overture, op. 115, in C major


440   "Nelson Mass" (also, "Imperial Mass"; "Missa in
      Angustiis")
      Haydn.  Mass in D minor  (Hob. XXII, 11)

      According to the autograph Ms. in the National Li-
brary, Vienna, this mass was composed in 1708 at Eisen-
stadt, within a period of 53 days.   During the time that
Haydn was working on it, news of the Battle of the Nile arrived.   The striking use of the trumpets in the Benedictus
is usually thought to be associated with the news of Nelson's
decisive victory.   After Haydn's death, a chart of the Battle
of the Nile was found among his papers, which strengthens
the belief that Haydn wrote it for Lord Nelson.


441   "Nicolaimesse" (also, "St. Joseph Mass")
      Haydn.  Mass in G major  (Hob. XXII, 6)

      In Austria this mass is affectionately called "Nicolai-
messe, " probably because Haydn wrote it for the Name Day
of Prince Nikolaus Esterházy on December 6, 1772.   It is

not at all a distinguished work, but rather gives the impression of being hastily tossed off. Haydn's own catalog of his works calls it St. Joseph Mass. Also known as Six-Four Time Mass (see no. 591).


442 "Night" (see "La Notte")
    Vivaldi. Concerto for Bassoon, String and Harpsichord
    in B♭ major (F. VIII, 1)


443 "The Night Moth"
    Chopin. Prelude, op. 28 no. 10, in C♯ minor (Brown
    123, no. 10)

Each of the Op. 28 preludes of Chopin was given a subtitle by Hans von Bülow, who commented on this one, "A night moth is flying around the room--there! it has suddenly hidden itself (the sustained G sharp); only its wings twitch a little. In a moment it takes flight anew and again settles down in darkness--its wings flutter (trill in the left hand). This happens several times, but at the last, just as the wings begin to quiver again, the busybody who lives in the room aims a stroke at the poor insect--it twitches once ... and dies" [Musician, xvi (1911)].


444 "Night Music" [Nacht Musique]
    Mozart. Serenade No. 12 in C minor (K. 388)

The character of this serenade, subtitled "Night Music," is completely different from the others. It is not light entertaining music, but rather somber in mood. All of it except the closing C major section, is in the minor key. Mozart probably wrote it for his musician friends in Vienna, either for them to perform or listen to. In a letter to his father dated July 27, 1782, Mozart himself referred to his serenade as "Nacht Musique" [sic].


445 "Night Music of the Streets of Madrid" [La Musica
        Notturna delle Strade di Madrid]
    Luigi Boccherini. Quintet for Two Violins, Viola and
        Two Cellos in C major, op. 30 no. 6 (Gérard 324)

The subtitle for this quintet was given to it by Boccherini in a note placed at the head of the quintet and faithfully reproduced by Picquot (in Italian) in his copy of the autograph (here translated).

"The night music of the streets of Madrid.   This
Quintettino describes the music that one hears, at night, in
the streets of Madrid, beginning with the bell of the Ave
Maria and ending with a military retreat...." The last
movement, "Retreat of Madrid with Variations," was a great
favorite of Boccherini's and he arranged it for other combinations:  one of these for piano, two violins, viola and
cello became part of a piano quintet, another part of a
double viola quintet for two violins two violas and one cello,
and still another for guitar, two violins, viola and cello.


446   "1933" (Nineteen Thirty-Three)
      Roy Harris.   Symphony No. 1

      Nicolas Slonimsky [Music Since 1900, p.  373] explains
that this first symphony was subtitled "1933" by the composer.   It was first performed by the Boston Symphony Orchestra January 26, 1934 and the following is a portion of
Harris' program notes.   "In the first movement I have tried
to capture the mood of adventure and physical exuberance;
in the second, of pathos which seems to underlie all human
existence; in the third, the mood of a positive will to power
and action. "


447   "The Nordic"
      Howard Hanson.   Symphony No. 1, op. 21, in E minor

      The composer intended the symphony to express some-
thing of the spirit of his Swedish ancestors who came to
America to settle in the midwest.   The movements are also
subtitled:  1. "Morning in the Hills"; 2. "Camp Meeting";
3. "Lazy Afternoon"; and 4. "Saturday Night. "


448   "Norse"
      MacDowell.   Sonata for Piano, op. 57 no. 3, in D
      minor

      The subtitle is best explained in the following lines
which the composer wrote at the beginning of the music:
"Night had fallen on a day of deed/ The great rafters in the
red-ribbed hall/ Flashed crimson in the fitful flame/ Of
smoldering logs;/ And from the stealthy shadows/ That
crept round Harold's throne/ Rang out a Skald's strong
voice/ With tales of battles won/ Of Gudrun's loves and
Sigurd, Siegmund's son. "

449   "North, East, South, West"
      Henry Hadley.   Symphony No. 4, op. 64, in D minor

In the four movements of this symphony, the composer
assigned each one to a different point of the compass.
"North" is an Allegro energico preceded by a Lento grave;
"East" is an Andante dolorosamente orientally colored;
"South" a Scherzo almost like ragtime in character; "West"
a brilliant final Allegro.   The work was written and first
performed for the Norfolk (Connecticut) Festival, June 5,
1911.


450   "Northern Symphony"
      Arnold Bax.   Symphony No. 3

This symphony received its subtitle because of its
somber tone color.   It is only in the beautiful epilogue that
there seems to be a peaceful resolution to the bitter and
troubled spirit of the North.


451   "Notre Amitié Est Invariable" [our friendship is un-
         changeable]
      Schubert.   Rondo for Piano Duet in D major, op. 128
         (D. 608)

The subtitle of this piece seems to refer to Schubert's
Hungarian friend, Josef von Gahy, his favorite partner in
playing piano four hands.   Einstein [Schubert, p. 153] remarks, "This friendship is perfectly symbolized in the bal-
ance of the partnership.   It is typical of Schubert's sly
sense of humor that he set this Rondo for Gahy--who liked
to play Schubert's dances in a manner calculated to galvanize
the dancers--in the form of a true Polonaise. "


452   "La Notte" [Night]
      Vivaldi.   Concerto in B♭ major for Bassoon and
         Strings   (F. VIII, 1)

The subtitle becomes clear when we examine the titles
of the various movements:   I. "Largo"; II. "Presto" (I
Fantasmi [the phantoms], full of disquiet and anxiety); III.
"Presto"; IV. "Andante molto" (Il Sonno [sleep]); and V.
"Allegro" (Sorge l'aurora [Sunrise]).

453   "Notturno"
      Mozart.   Serenade no.  8 in D major   (K. 286)

This piece was written for four orchestras, or rather
for one orchestra of strings and horns, answered by three
other orchestras in a triple echo.   Einstein comments, "If
we didn't have reason to believe that it was composed for
New Year's Day, 1777, we should say that it was the proper
nocturnal music for the baroque curiosities at Mirabell Garden, near Salzburg   But Mozart was fond of conjuring up
summertime in the winter" [Mozart, p. 208].


454   "Die Nullte" ("No. 0")
      Bruckner.   Symphony No. Zero in D minor

This symphony has been dubbed "Die Nullte" ("No. 0")
according to many writers, including Bruckner's pupil and
friend August Göllerich.   The work was composed in 1864,
two years before the first symphony.   That is the reason
for its nickname.
      It is an experience to hear this symphony today
even though the self-critical Bruckner had wanted to sup-
press it.   Its introduction to the record catalogue allows
collectors to sample the master's style at an early and particularly self-revealing stage.


455   "Ocean"
      Chopin.   Etude for Piano, op. 25 no. 12, in C minor
      (Brown 99, No. 12)

This etude has for years been nicknamed "Ocean" and
with good reason.   The arpeggios sweep up and down the
keyboard, giving the effect of the tremendous power of the
tides of the ocean.


456   "Ocean"
      Anton Rubinstein.   Symphony No. 2, in C major

During Rubinstein's lifetime this symphony was known
by its nickname all over the world.   It was originally written in four movements but Rubinstein added two more.   In
two instances the critic Ambros compared this symphony
with Beethoven's "Pastorale."
      First he compared the so-called "Sailor's Dance" in

the "Ocean" to the "Peasant's Merrymaking" in the "Pastorale," and then the final choral in the Rubinstein work
to the "glad and grateful tidings after the storm" in the
Beethoven.  In Ambros' criticism, he also alluded to Rubinstein's good taste in leaving the storm on the "Ocean" to
the discretion of the listeners.  Perhaps it is this very
thought that gave the symphony its nickname.


457   "Ochsenmenuett"  (see "Ox Minuet")
      I. X. Seyfried; attrib to Haydn.  Minuet for Orchestra
      (Hob.  IX, 27)


458   "The October Symphony"
      Shostakovich.  Symphony No. 2, op. 14

      This symphony was inspired by the month in which the
Bolshevik Revolution occurred and is celebrated.  The title
page of the score reads, "Dm. Shostakovich op. 14.  To
October, A Symphonic dedication with a closing story written to the words of A. Bezimensky for Large Orchestra and
Mixed Chorus."  On the top right hand corner of the page
are the words "Proletarians of the World Unite!"
      On November 6, 1927, the "October Symphony" was
performed by the Leningrad Philharmonic at a concert celebrating the tenth anniversary of the Bolshevik Revolution.


459   "On the Departure of a Beloved Brother" [Sopra la
      Lontananza d'un Fratello Diletto]
      J. S. Bach.  Capriccio in B♭ major for Piano  (BWV
      992)

      This is a vivid piece of program music which Bach
wrote in Arnstadt about 1704, to mark the departure of his
brother, Johann Jakob, as oboist in the Swedish service.
In a short fugal movement Johann Jakob's friends try to
describe the dangers ahead.  Then their lamentations are
heard, only to be disturbed by the sounds of the postilion's
horn, and finally the coach goes off, to a brisk entertaining
fugue.
      Parry does not hesitate to call this, "The most
dexterous piece of the kind that had ever appeared in the
world up to that time."

460   "On The Shore"   (see "Songs Without Words")
      Mendelssohn.   Piece for Piano, op. 53 no. 1, in A♭
      major


461   "Organ Solo Mass"
      Mozart.   Mass in C major   (K. 259)

   In a letter Mozart's father wrote 18 months after Mozart had written the Mass in C, he referred to it as "Wolfgang's Mass with the Organ Solo. " The reason for this is
the important organ solo in the Benedictus.   The first performance of the "Organ Solo Mass" was at the consecration
of the Archbishop of Olmütz in Salzburg in 1788.


462   "Organ Symphony"
      Saint-Saëns.   Symphony No. 3 in C minor, op. 78

   Saint-Saëns had held several very important posts as
organist, and when he wrote his Third Symphony that instrument was uppermost in his mind; thenceforth it has always
been referred to as the "Organ Symphony. " It had its first
performance at a concert of the London Philharmonic Society
in 1886 and was said to be Saint-Saëns' instrumental master-
piece.


463   "Our Friendship Is Unchangeable"   (see "Notre Amitié
         Est Invariable")
      Schubert.   Rondo for Piano Duet in D major, op. 138
         (D. 608)


464   "L'Ours"   (see "The Bear")
      Haydn.   Symphony No. 82 in C major   (Hob. I, 82)


465   "Ox Minuet" [Ochsenmenuett]
      I. X. Seyfried; attrib to Haydn.   Minuet for Orchestra
         (Hob. IX, 27)

   Frederick Crowest [Musical Anecdotes, v. 1, p. 173]
relates the following anecdote, supposed to explain the origin
of the nickname:   A butcher called on Haydn in Vienna and,
after complimenting him profusely, of Haydn's music, was
to be married, and her greatest wish was to have Haydn

write a piece of music for the occasion. Haydn, kind as
ever complied with the request, and the next day the butcher
received the minuet. Haydn would have thought the incident
ended, had he not been surprised a few days later to hear
the music of the minuet being played outside his house. He
hastened to the window, and looking down, was amazed to
see a huge ox, with gilded horns and wonderful decorations,
surrounded by a street orchestra. The butcher went up to
Haydn and said, "Dear Sir, I thought that a butcher could
not express his gratitude in a more becoming manner than
by offering you the finest ox in his possession. "

There is another completely different explanation of
the "Ox Minuet": This is often taken for the familiar name
of one of Haydn's Minuets, but the actual one is not known.
In 1832 Ignaz Xavier Seyfried wrote a Singspiel with music
taken from Haydn's works, with the title of "Die Ochsen-
Menuette. " However, he did not borrow this minuet. Also,
sometime earlier, there were two stage pieces with music
selected from Haydn, produced at Verdun (1805) called
"Le Menuet du Boeuf; ou, Une Leçon de Haydn. "

466   "Oxford Symphony"
      Haydn.   Symphony No. 92 in G major   (Hob. I, 92)

When Oxford conferred an honorary degree of Doctor
of Music on Haydn in 1791, he composed a new symphony
for the occasion. However, the orchestra did not have time
to rehearse the new one and instead played the composer's
Symphony No. 92 in G major, which has always been known
as the "Oxford Symphony. "

467   "Paganini Rhapsody"
      Rachmaninoff.   Rhapsody on a Theme of Paganini, op.
      43

Rachmaninoff uses the theme of Paganini's 24th Caprice
for his so called "Paganini Rhapsody. " The theme is faintly
suggested in the nine-measure orchestral introduction, but
is played in its entirety by the violins in the first Variation.

There are 24 variations in all, mostly short and
contrasting in mood and treatment. In three of the variations, there is the addition of a somber theme from the
Dies Irae, that portion of the Catholic Requiem Mass for the
dead which comments on the Day of Judgment.

468    "Paganini Variations"
       Brahms.   Variations on a Theme of Paganini, op. 35,
       in A minor

       There are two books consisting of 30 variations that
Brahms wrote on a 12-bar passage of Paganini.   Each variation exhausts a technical problem in character and style
"à la Paganini. "   Clara Schumann was quite right in refer-
ring to them as "Witch Variations" ["Hexen-Variationen"].


469    "Paganiniana"
       Alfredo Casella.   Divertimento for Orchestra, op. 65

       This has been subtitled "Paganiniana" by the composer
because he based his orchestral work on themes of Paganini.
The opening movement is based on four of the caprices for
solo violin.   The second movement, the Polachetta (Little
Polonaise) is taken from a quartet for violin, viola, cello
and guitar.   The third movement "Romanza" is from a still
unpublished work for violin and orchestra which Casella discovered in a private music library at Mannheim.   The fourth,
or "Tarantelle," is from another unpublished work of Paganini.   [From Philadelphia Orchestra program notes, November 13, 1967. ]


470    "The Palindrome"
       Haydn.   Symphony No. 47 in G major   (Hob. I, 47)

       The subtitle comes from the third movement, "Menuet
al Roverso, " which again speaks for Haydn's love for ex-
periment.   As in a palindrome, a word or word sequence
which reads the same backwards as forwards, the second
half of the Minuet is obtained by playing the first half backwards.   The trio is similarly constructed.


471    "Paris Symphonies"
       Haydn.   Symphonies Nos. 82-87   (Hob. I, 82-87)

       In 1786 Haydn was commissioned to write six sym-
phonies for the fashionable Parisian concert organization,
"Les Concerts de la Loge Olympique. "   The set has always
been referred to as the "Paris Symphonies" and is as follows:   No. 82 in C major ("L'Ours"); No. 83 in G minor
("La Poule"); No. 84 in E♭ major; No. 85 in B♭ major
("La Reine"); No. 86 in D major; and No. 87 in A major.

472   "Paris Symphony"
      Mozart.  Symphony No. 31 in D major  (K. 297)

    When Mozart was in Paris with his mother in the sum-
mer of 1778, he was commissioned by Le Gros, the director of the Concerts Spirituels, to compose a symphony for
the opening of the Corpus Christi program.  His Symphony
in D, nicknamed the "Paris Symphony" was written for the
occasion.
    As Mozart was particularly anxious to please Paris,
he wrote witty and charming music that would meet the
musical taste of the day.  The symphony had no menuet, no
repeats.  When Le Gros objected to the slow movement as
"Too long and too full of modulations," Mozart obligingly
provided another one.  (The second and shorter Andante
was published in Paris, but the original one is included in
the full Breitkopf und Härtel edition, and is the one usually
performed).


473   "Passion"  (see "Songs Without Words")
      Mendelssohn.  Piece for Piano, op. 85 no. 3, in E♭
        major


474   "La Passione"
      Haydn.  Symphony No. 49 in F minor  (Hob. I, 49)

    The subtitle of this symphony definitely suggests that
the performance of the work was to be during Holy Week.
Musically the symphony is the climax of Haydn's efforts to
give depth of feeling to his symphonies.  There are few
works of the 18th century that surpass this one in the
dramatic intensity of expression.


475   "Pastoral"
      Colin McPhee.  Symphony No. 2

    The composer writes this about the subtitle:  "The
work depends on natural lyrical development rather than
planned abstract form.  The melodic material is in part
original, in part developed from Balinese pentatonic melodic fragments.  In mood and orchestral texture it is inspired by a pastoral or rural scene of no locale.

"It seemed to several friends, after hearing the
test pressing, that something needed to be added to the title
to give some clue to the character of the work; pastoral
immediately sprang to mind, but I had not the courage for
'Pastorale Symphony.' Hence the subtitle 'Pastoral'...."

476  "Pastoral"
Alan Rawsthorne.  Symphony No. 2

David Ewen [World of 20th Century Music, p. 638]
states that the Second Symphony reveals the romantic facet
of the composer's many-sided creative personality.  The
composer has explained that this music sprang from the
various sensations aroused by life in the country.  That
is why he subtitled it "Pastoral."

477  "Pastoral"
Vaughan Williams.  Symphony No. 3

The symphony, labeled "Pastoral," depicts a philosophical approach to nature.  In Simona Pakenham's fine
book, Ralph Vaughan Williams, there is the following apt
description of the work: "It is as if the composer, coming
back from the years of war and noise and the constant com-
panionship of army life, had suddenly found himself alone
among the hills around his home in a silence so grateful
and profound that as well as the bird-song and the wind,
he could hear the stirring of the sap in the trees and the
movement of the roots under the earth" [p. 58].

478  "Pastorale"
Beethoven.  Sonata for Piano, op. 28, in D major

When this sonata was published in 1838, by Cranz of
Hamburg, he gave it the not too inappropriate nickname
"Pastorale."  The autograph of the sonata bears the inscription, "Gran Sonata op. 28 1801 da L. v. Beethoven."  The
cadence theme of the first movement and the main theme of
the Rondo are somewhat "volkstümlich" in character.
Another possibility as to the nickname may be the overall
sunny character of the music.

479  "Pastorale"
Beethoven.  Symphony No. 6, op. 68, in F major

The autograph of this symphony has the following note in Beethoven's hand: "Angenehme heitre Empfindungen welche bey der Ankunft auf dem Lande im Menschen erwachen" [pleasant, cheerful feelings which arise in man on arriving in the country]. Elliott Forbes has pointed out that the first use of the word "Pastoral" is in connection with a violin part used at the first performance, which reads "Sinfonia Pastorella, Pastoral-Sinfonie oder Erinnerung an das Landleben. Mehr Ausdruck der Empfindung als Mahlerei" [memories of country life. More an expression of feeling than painting]. The work was composed in the neighborhood of Vienna, in the beautiful country between Heiligenstadt and Grinzing and completed in the summer of 1808.

John N. Burk says, "One can imagine the composer dreaming away lazy hours in the summer heat at Döbling or Grinzing, lingering in the woods, by a stream or at a favorite tavern, while the gentle droning themes of the symphony hum in his head, taking limpid shapes" [Works of Beethoven, p. 282].

480  "Pastorale"
     Scarlatti.  Sonata for Piano in C major  (L. 53, K.
       513)

Ralph Kirpatrick [Domenico Scarlatti, p. 203] writes the following about this piece:  "The bagpipes of the southern Italian zampognari with the droning basses and lilting Christmas tunes of the pifferari are always to be heard in those pieces to which Scarlatti himself gives the subtitle "Pastorale."

481  "La Pastorella" [the shepherdess]
     Vivaldi.  Concerto in D major for Flute, Oboe, Violin,
       Bassoon and Continuo  (F. XII, 29)

482  "Pater Dominicus" (or, "Dominicus")
     Mozart.  Mass in C major  (K. 66)

When Mozart was only 13 years old he wrote his first high mass, the so-called "Pater Dominicus" or "Dominicus." Mozart wrote it for the ordination of Cajetan Hagenauer, a son of Lorenz Hagenauser, the landlord of the Mozart family.  Cajetan had entered the Benedictine Monastery while the Mozarts were on their grand tour, and on October 15, 1769 he celebrated, as "Pater Dominicus," his first high mass.


483   "Pathétique"
      Beethoven.   Sonata for Piano, op. 13, in C minor

There are two different stories of this famous sonata, as related by Tovey [A Companion..., p. 68]: (1) The first edition of this sonata, which appeared in 1799, bore the sub-title, "Grande Sonate Pathétique." We have reason to believe that this was given by Beethoven, or at least sanctioned by him.

    Early in 1798, at the age of 28, Beethoven came to the terrifying and shattering realization that he was growing increasingly deaf. At first regarding this defect as a shameful malady, he withdrew completely from society, but he was soon to return through his music, music that grew in stature with each painstaking effort. Among the staggering number of pages that began to flow from his pen was this "Pathétique" Sonata.

    (2) The subtitle "Sonata Pathétique" was given to this work by the publisher, Eder. His justification was that nothing so powerful and full of tragic passion had ever been dreamed of in piano music. "The Sonata Pathétique, like the Kreutzer Sonata (a less consistent work, akin to it in many ways) begins with a magnificent piece of Homeric fighting; but if we overestimate the tragic quality of such fighting, we shall end, like Tolstoy, in crassly underestimating the rest" [p. 68].


484   "Pathétique"
      Tchaikovsky.   Symphony No. 6 in B minor

    Talking with his brother, Modeste, the day after the first performance of the Sixth Symphony, Tchaikovsky discussed the problem of a subtitle, for he was about to send the score to the publisher. He thought of calling it "A Programme Symphony," and had written to his nephew, Vladimir Davidoff, about it. After giving it some more thought he foresaw that to give it such a name would explain nothing, and at the same time might invite questions which he could not answer.

    He finally accepted Modeste's suggestion of "Pathétique" and sent it off to Jurgenson, the publisher, only to

regret that decision and write again suggesting his prefer-
ence for using only the number of the symphony.  However,
it was too late and the symphony was published as "Pathétique. "  Evidently Jurgenson thought that a good "selling"
name.


485   "Paukenmesse"  (see 'Kettledrum Mass")
      Haydn.  Mass in C major  (Hob. XXII, 9)


486   "Peacock Variations"
      Kodály.  Variations on a Hungarian Folksong

      David Ewen [in World of 20th Century Music, p. 428]
explains that Zoltán Kodály wrote these orchestral variations
to help celebrate the 50th anniversary of the Concertgebouw
Orchestra in Amsterdam which introduced it on November
23, 1939 with Wilhelm Mengelberg conducting.  The American concert premiere took place under the composers' direction during his first visit to the United States in Philadelphia, November 22, 1946.
      The reason for the subtitle was that the entire work
is based on the folk melody "Fly, Peacock, Fly," which
comes from the district of Somogy at the western end of
Lake Balaton, Hungary.


487   "Peasant Cantata" [Bauern-Cantate]
      J. S. Bach.  Mer Hahn en neue Oberkeet--Cantata 212
      (BWV 212)

      The cantata, "Mer Hahn en Neue Oberkeet," popularly
known as the "Peasant Cantata," was written to celebrate
Carl Heinrich von Dieskau's coming into possession of land.
The ceremonial performance was held on August 30, 1742.
      Picander, who wrote the text, held a post under von
Dieskau at the Customs House in Leipzig.  To give local
color to the words Picander used the patois of Upper Saxony,
and Bach, in writing the music, introduced popular melodies,
among them the familiar sarabande "Folies d'Espagne. "
This popularization of the work has no doubt given it its
nickname.


488   "The Philosopher"
      Haydn.  Symphony No. 22 in E♭ major  (Hob. I, 22)

The grave seriousness of the opening of the Adagio with the solemn notes of the canto fermo by horns and English horns (replacing the oboes) is said to have given the symphony its nickname.


489   "Philosophic"
      Bruckner.   Symphony No. 6 in A major

When Bruckner was writing his Sixth Symphony, he was going through a difficult period of his life.   He was lonely, ill and had many financial problems.   In spite of all this, the first movement, from which the nickname supposedly originates, is extremely cheerful.
      It is said that Bruckner liked to speak of his Sixth Symphony as the "keckste" [most daring] referring, of course, to certain formal and harmonic features of the work.   However, the more apt and more widely used nickname, "Philosophic," is very fitting because the work is an eloquent expression of the resignation that had come over Bruckner's soul.


490   "Phoebus and Pan"
      J. S. Bach.   Der Streit zwischen Phoebus und Pan--
          Cantata 201   (BWV 201)

Bach wrote this work with the same intention as Wagner wrote his Meistersinger.   The characters in the cantata are: Phoebus, Pan, Momus, Mercurius, and Midas.   In the character of Midas, the counterpart of Beckmesser, Bach attacks a recent and unfriendly critic of his music. Phoebus (Bach) challenged by Pan, engages in a contest of song with him.   Midas declares Pan the victor and is punished with a "pair of ass's ears" and relegated to the back woods.   The cantata is usually referred to by its popular name, "Phoebus and Pan," and really belongs to the category of burlesque satire.


491   "Il Piacere" [Pleasure]
      Vivaldi.   Concerto in C major for Violin, Strings and
          Organ   (F. I, 27)


492   "The Pilgrims"   (see "Songs Without Words").
      Mendelssohn.   Piece for Piano, op. 67 no. 3, in B♭
          major

493    "The Pioneer"
       G. F. Bristow.    Arcadian Symphony No. 4 in F♯ mi-
       nor, op. 49

George Frederic Bristow, a native New Yorker, was
born in Brooklyn in 1825 and died in New York City in 1898.
He gave his Fourth Symphony its subtitle because in this
work he suggests the vicissitudes of the pioneer.   The four
movements are "Allegro Appassionata"; "Adagio"; "Indian
War Dance"; and "Allegro con Spirito. "

494    "Pizzicato"
       Bruckner.    Symphony No. 5 in B♭ major

It is because of the plucked string background throughout this work that the nickname has been popularly but ir-
relevantly used.

495    "Les Plaintives"
       Chopin.    Nocturnes, op. 27    (Brown 91, 96)

496    "A Pleasure Boat"
       Chopin.    Prelude, op. 28 no. 23, in F major    (Brown
       107, no. 23)

Each of the Op. 28 preludes of Chopin was given a
subtitle by Hans von Bülow, who wrote about this one, "A
gaily decked boat glides over the mirror-like surface of the
water; flags and pennants wave in the breeze, streamers
flutter (arpeggio figure in the right hand, trill in the left).
It sails farther and farther away; it can be seen only as a
mere speck in the distance.   We can barely discern the
flag; it flutters--now it has disappeared" [Musician, xvi
(1911)].

497    "The Poem of Ecstasy" [Poème de l'Extase]
       Scriabin.    Sonata No. 5, op. 53, in F♯ major

Faubion Bowers tells us that Scriabin was inspired to
write this immediately after completion of the Symphony No.
4, the "Poème de l'Extase. "   Scriabin said that the Fifth
Sonata came from somewhere outside of himself.   He "saw"
it in a flash of inspiration and struggled to write it down as

quickly as possible.    Because of this he subtitled the sonata
with the title of his symphony.    [Scriabin, v. II, p. 182].


498    "Poème Mystique"
        Bloch.    Sonata No. 2 for Violin and Piano

        The idea of this sonata was supposed to have come to
Ernest Bloch in a dream and perhaps this is what suggested
the subtitle to him    The composer had written to Alex
Cohen, the foremost authority on his chamber music in
England, that he had thought of writing a Sonata of Faith
and Serenity and that the dream was the "ignition spark. "


499    "Polish"
        Tchaikovsky.    Symphony No. 3 in D major

        Weinstock calls this symphony a "symphonic grab-bag
full of five sketchy and tenuously related movements. "    It
is from the fifth movement, the Tempo de Polacca, that the
nickname "Polish" originates.    However, it lacks the brilliant local color of the Polish scenes, as we have them in
the nationalistic opera, "A Life for the Tsar. "


500    "Polish Ballade"
        Chopin.    Ballade for Piano, op. 23 no. 1, in G minor
          (Brown 66)

        According to Brown's Thematic Catalogue this work is
often referred to as the "Polish Ballade. "


501    "The Polish Dance"
        Chopin.    Prelude, op. 28 no. 7, in A major    (Brown
          100, no. 7)

        Each of the Op. 28 preludes of Chopin was given a
subtitle by Hans von Bülow.    His description of this one is:
"We see a girl dancing in the Polish manner; that is, lifting
the feet but slightly and carrying through her dance more by
swaying and graceful movements than by actual steps.    It
is the poetry of the dance" [Musician, xvi (1911)].

502    "Polonaise Héroique"
       Chopin.    Polonaise for Piano, op. 53, in A♭ major
          (Brown 147)

The strong, almost martial rhythm of the Polonaise in
A♭ major, may be taken to represent the feudal court of
Poland in the days of all its splendor.    It may be this
quality that has given the piece its nickname.


503    "La Posiana" [the woman from Posen]
       Chopin.    Rondo in F major for Piano, op. 5    (Brown
          15)


504    "Post Horn"
       Mozart.    Serenade No. 9 in D major    (K. 320)

In the second Minuet of this Serenade, there is a humorous quotation of the four natural notes of the then familiar
post horn, and undoubtedly Mozart's deliberate intention of
parodying the post horn has given the piece its nickname.


505    "La Poule"    (see "The Hen")
       Haydn.    Symphony No. 83 in G minor    (Hob. I, 83)


506    "Prague"
       Mozart.    Symphony No. 38 in D major    (K. 504)

Although this symphony was finished in Vienna on December 6, 1786, there is the feeling that Mozart was think-
ing of his forthcoming trip to Prague--where it received its
first performance on January 9, 1787--when he wrote it.
       The story is that the symphony was an immediate
success and that the applause was so loud and so long that
the audience would not be appeased until Mozart improvised
on the piano for over half an hour.    Finally someone in the
audience shouted "Figaro."    Mozart improvised variations
on the air "Non Più Andrai" and that satisfied the clamoring
crowd.


507    "Presentiment of Death"
       Chopin.    Prelude, op. 28 no. 2, in A minor for Piano
          (Brown 123, no. 2)

Each of the Op. 28 preludes of Chopin was given a
subtitle by Hans von Bülow, who wrote of this one: "This
is an uncertain in character as in key: it begins in E minor, goes into G major; then to B minor, only to lose itself slowly in A minor.  The mood is constantly changing,
yet it always comes back to one and the same thought, the
melancholy tolling of a funeral knell.  The two-voiced accompaniment in the left hand is difficult to play legato.  In
the right hand one [h]ears the inexorable voice of death,
though toward the end it falters and loses the measure in
uncertain tones, as if saying, 'He comes not, the deliverer!
It was a delusion. ' This is what the questioning end seems
to say" [Musician, xvi (1911)].


508   "The Prophets"
      Castelnuovo-Tedesco.   Concerto No. 2 for Violin

     The composer writes the following concerning this
work: "'The Prophets' was supposed to be the title (and
not the subtitle) of my second Violin Concerto; my first
Violin Concerto had (as a title) 'Concerto Italiano' because
it expressed the lyrical, Italian (almost post Vivaldi) side
of my nature; and when Heifetz asked me to write another
one I told him that I would like this time to express 'the
other side' of my nature and my education--the Jewish one--
so I called it 'The Prophets' and I even gave subtitles to
the three individual movements, Isaiah, Jeremiah, and Elijah,
but Heifetz wanted something more 'generic' so 'The Prophets' became the subtitle and the piece was known as 'Concerto No. 2'. "


509   "Il Proteo o sia il Mondo al Rovescio" [Proteus, or
         the world topsy-turvy]
      Vivaldi.   Concerto in F major for Violin, Cello,
         Strings and Harpsichord   (F. IV, 5)


510   "The Prussian Quartets"
      Haydn.   Six String Quartets, op. 50   (Hob III, 44-49)

     These quartets were dedicated to Wilhelm II, King of
Prussia, and have always been known as "The Prussian
Quartets. " Number six of this group is also known by its
nickname "Der Frosch" [the Frog--which see].

511    "Quartetto Dorico"
       Respighi.   String Quartet in D major

In Beethoven's Quartet Op. 132, the Lydian mode is
used for the famous song of thanksgiving on recovery from
an illness, so that modal flavor is not unprecedented in a
chamber work.   However, the mode used as a basis for an
entire score, as the Dorian mode is used in this one, is
somewhat more venturesome.   Because of this, Ottorino
Respighi understandably subtitled the piece "Quartetto Dorico" [Dorian Quartet].


512    "Quartetto Serioso"
       Beethoven.   String Quartet, op. 95, in F minor

The autograph manuscript of this quartet preserved in
the National Library at Vienna bears the inscription, "Quartetto Serioso 1810 in the month of October dedicated to
Herr von Zmeskall and written in the month of October by
his friend L. v. Beethoven. "  The music is serious and
somber throughout.   Even the third movement, which is
scherzo in form, has the marking, "Allegro assai Vivace,
ma serioso. "


513    "Quartettsatz"
       Schubert.   String Quartet No. 12 in C minor   (D. 703)

In December 1820 Schubert turned to quartet writing
again but his single chamber music work of that year remained unfinished.   The nickname "Quartettsatz" [literally,
"quartet movement"] also called "Satz Quartet," which is
bad German for "Quartettsatz") refers to the first movement in C minor and a fragment of second movement.
       "Here a new Schubert stands before us.   The inner
joy and vivacity which filled the earlier works is gone, a
restlessness and concern with more serious expression appears.   A tortured twisting chromatic theme is passed
about from instrument to instrument, over rapidly shifting
harmonies.   The second theme, more songful, offers but
little relief from the dissatisfaction expressed by the first.
With this C minor movement, peace of mind and joy of
spirit ceased to be typical components of Schubert's chamber music" [p. 291].

514   "The Quinten"
      Haydn.   String Quartet, op. 76 no. 2, in D minor
      (Hob. III, 76)

The nickname is derived from the descending fifths (in
German, "Quinten") in the first movement.   This quartet is
also known as "The Bell" and sometimes "The Donkey."
The falling fifths have evidently suggested a bell-peal to
some and the hee-haw of a donkey to others.

515   "La Quintette de la Balle" [Quintet of the bullet]
      George Onslow.   Quintet for Strings No. 15 in C minor

In 1829 the composer had had an accident at a wolf
hunt where a bullet hit him in the face making him somewhat deaf in one ear for the rest of his life.   He wrote this
string quintet, which he himself subtitled, to describe the
pain he had suffered during his illness and to show his gratitude on recovering.

516   "The Rage Over a Lost Penny" [Die Wut über den ver-
      lornen Groschen ausgetobt in einer Caprice]
      Beethoven.   Capriccio for Piano, op. 129, in G major

Robert Schumann says of this composition: "It would
be difficult to find anything merrier than this whim.   This
was a moment for Beethoven to use his favorite expression
when he was inwardly merry.   'Today I feel altogether un-
buttoned' and then he laughed like a lion and beat about him,
for he was always untamable.   'But with this Capriccio I'll
get you'" [Music and Musicians, p. 105].
      It was published as Rondo a Capriccio by Diabelli in
Vienna in 1828.   The opus number (129) was not given to it
until sometime later.   Beethoven's title on the autograph
was, "Leichte Kaprice alla ungharese quasi un capriccio"
[light caprice in a Hungarian style like a capriccio].   The
popular title (in German) appears on the autograph in an un-
identified hand.
      The autograph brought a high price at the auction of
Beethoven's estate and belonged successively to the publishers C. A. Spina and Heinrich Schlesinger.   Sold again in
London in 1925, it disappeared until found by Otto E. Albrecht in Providence, R. I., in the collection of Mrs. Eugene Allen Noble in 1942.   It was acquired in 1973 by
Robert O. Lehman of New York.

517   "Rain Sonata" ("Regen-Sonate")
      Brahms.   Sonata for Violin and Piano, op. 78, in G
      major

In the last movement of the Sonata Op. 78, Brahms
uses his song "Regenlied" [Rain Song], Op. 59, No. 3,
which was written to the following text by Claus Groth:
"Walle, Regen; walle nieder/ Wecke meine alten Lieder/
Die wir in der Türe sangen/ Wenn die Tropfen draussen
klangen!/ Möchte ihnen wieder lauschen/ Ihrem süssen,
feuchten Rauschen/ Meine Seele sanft betauen/ Mit dem
frommen Kindergrauen" [steam down, rain; awaken my old
song, which we used to sing at the door when the drops were
pattering outside.   Would that I could listen to you again,
hear your sweet plashing, and steep my soul softly in the
holy awe of childhood].
      The incessant running figure of the piano part cer-
tainly suggests the gentle patter of rain, but the origin of
the popular title "Rain Sonata" comes as a result of the
thematic quotation.


518   "Raindrop"
      Chopin.   Prelude for Piano, op. 28 no. 15, in D♭
      major   (Brown 107, no. 15)

This prelude was supposed to have been written while
rain was falling on the roof of the Monastery of Valldemosa.
Chopin denied that this had influenced him but his companion
George Sand, seemed to think that it had done so without
his realizing it.
      The music does create the impression of gently fall-
ing rain, which in the middle section becomes ominous only
to fade away into a patter of rain.   Hans von Bülow, who
gave subtitles to each of Chopin's Op. 28 preludes, comments on No. 15: "The tones on A flat, which later changes
to G sharp, should be played with the utmost uniformity,
dynamic as well as rhythmic; there are no uneven drops.
The melody only calls for expression.   The mood of the
second section, though heavy and sultry, is still quiet in the
main.   The wind howls down the chimney (C sharp minor),
the storm draws nearer, the lightning flashes--it strikes (E
major); while the rain falls in torrents.   It grows dark--it
lightens, it thunders, the rain beats through the roof; one
can hear it forcing its way through various crevices (the
repeated notes change).   While still dripping it begins to
clear (enharmonic change from G sharp to A flat).   The first

melody reappears--now the drops suddenly cease to fall;
they are heard only in imagination (count two eighth notes to
a quarter with scrupulous exactness).   Light in hand, Chopin
searches to see if it is leaking; the water is still finding its
way inside.   Later, while all are sleeping, he hears it dripping in his dreams" [Musician, xvi (1911)].   Maurice Brown
has pointed out that the story would equally well fit Prelude
No. 6 in B minor, and indeed Liszt preferred to associate
the story with yet another, No. 8 in F sharp minor.


519   "The Rákóczy March"
      Liszt.   Hungarian Rhapsody for Piano No. 15 in A
      minor

    The Hungarian Rhapsody No. 15 is based on the famous
Rákóczy March.   When Prince Franz Rákóczy II had made
his entry into his capital of Eperjes, after having led the
revolt against Austria in early 1700, his favorite musician,
the court violinist Michael Barna, composed a march in his
honor.
    This Rákóczy March, full of temperament, sorrow
and pain, soon became popular among the music loving gyp-
sies, as well as among the Hungarian people.   The first
"Rákóczy March" came from Carl Vaczek of Jaszo in Hungary, who was a prominent dilettante in music.   He had
heard the march from a granddaughter of Barna, who was a
fine violinist.   Vaczek had written down the composition and
handed the manuscript to another violinist, Ruzsitska, who
in turn had altered it.
    The original melody by Barna remained the one pre-
ferred by the Hungarian people, but in the transcription of
Berlioz, perhaps the most famous one, the composition of
Ruzsitska was used.
    The interesting thing is that Liszt's arrangement of
the same march used in his Rhapsody No. 15 led to a de-
bate in the Hungarian Diet in which M. Tisza spoke of the
march as the work of Franz Rákóczy II.   This was incor-
rect.   Berlioz was also mistaken in saying that it was by an
unknown composer.   According to Lina Ramann, Liszt's
biographer, it was written by a military band master named
Scholl.   She also states that, although Liszt had made his
transcription in 1840, it was not published until 1870, out
of courtesy to Berlioz.

520   "Rasiermesser-Quartett"   (see "Razor Quartet")
      Haydn.   String Quartet in F minor, op. 55 no. 2
      (Hob. III, 61)


521   "Rasumovsky Quartets"
      Beethoven.   String Quartets, op. 59

Beethoven wrote the three Op. 59 quartets for his patron, the Russian nobleman, Count Rasumovsky, who had
requested quartets with Russian themes, original or imitated.
There are actual Russian folk songs quoted in the F and E
minor quartets, and a brooding slow movement in the C major one is said to be a transformed folk song.
      Count Rasumovsky was the Russian Ambassador to
Vienna, and during this period maintained a palace which
became the virtual center of the city's artistic life.   He
also put at Beethoven's disposal a quartet consisting of the
finest available players (the Count played second violin)
which met in the evenings and performed among other compositions, new works by Beethoven under the composer's
own direction.
      Thayer tells us [Life of L. v. Beethoven, v. II, p.
97] that the following interesting bit was found on one leaf
of 21 leaves of sketches to the Rasumovsky Quartets written
in pencil in Beethoven's hand:   "Even as you have plunged
into the whirlpool of society you will find it possible to
compose operas in spite of social obstacles.   Let your deafness no longer remain a secret not even in art. "


522   "Razor Quartet" [Rasiermesser]
      Haydn.   String Quartet, op. 55 no. 2, in F minor
      (Hob. III, 61)

A particularly enterprising publisher, John Bland, took
the trouble to travel from London to Esterháza to obtain new
works and to persuade Haydn to visit London.   Bland used
to tell an amusing story about how the master presented him
with the autograph of this quartet.
      When Bland visited Haydn, the master was shaving.
The razor must have been a dull one because Haydn ex-
claimed, "I would give my best quartet for a good razor!"
Bland, overhearing this, rushed to Haydn's room with his
own excellent set of razors; Haydn was delighted and kept
his promise.

523   "Reformation"
Mendelssohn.   Symphony No. 5 in D minor, op. 107

According to Radcliff [Mendelssohn, p. 22], when Mendelssohn composed his "Reformation" Symphony in North
Wales in September 1892, he had in mind the celebration
planned in Germany for the following year of the tercenten-
ary of the Augsburg Confession, the drawing up of the Con-
stitution of the Protestant faith in June, 1530.   In the introduction to the first movement, Mendelssohn used the so
called "Dresden Amen" otherwise known as the Eucharist
motif in Wagner's Parsifal.
At the completion of the symphony he sent it to his
sister Fanny, with the note, "Try to collect opinions as to
the title I ought to select--"Reformation Symphony," "Confession Symphony," "Symphony for a Church Festival," or
"Juvenile Symphony. "
Although Mendelssohn had decided to subtitle the
symphony, "Reformation," the name by which it has always
been known, the actual celebration for which he had written
it did not take place.   However, the composer was apparently relieved, because he wrote to Dorn in June, "Perhaps it
is well for some reasons that the performance has been
postponed, for it occurred to me afterwards that the chorale
part and the other Catholicisms would have a strange appearance in a theatre, and that the 'Reformation Song' would
not sound very well at Whitsuntide. "

524   "Regrets" (see "Songs Without Words")
Mendelssohn.   Piece for Piano, op. 19 no. 2, in A
minor

525   "La Reine" [the Queen]
Haydn.   Symphony No. 85 in B♭ major   (Hob. I, 85)

This symphony is one of a set of six that Haydn was
commissioned to write for the Parisian concert organization,
"Les Concerts de la Loge Olympique. "   Queen Marie An-
toinette was a frequent attender of these concerts and, because this particular symphony with its elegant and queenly
leisure was one of her favorites, it was nicknamed "La
Reine. "   The title first appears as "La Reine de France"
in the Imbault edition.

526   "Reiter-Quartett"   (see "The Rider")
      Haydn.   String Quartet in G minor, op. 74 no. 3
      (Hob. III, 73)


527   "Religious Meditation"
      Gottschalk.   The Last Hope--Piece for Piano, op. 16

      According to Jeanne Behrend's notes [in her ed. of
Piano Music of L. M. Gottschalk], this has been subtitled
"Religious Meditation" because it can be found in various
current hymnals.   In the silent movies it served to enhance
sentimental and religious scenes.   According to a French
music journal of the day Gottschalk called this work his
"Evening Prayer, " playing it every evening to the memory
of a Cuban lady whose last moments he had eased with its
improvisation.


528   "Reliquié"   (see "Unfinished")
      Schubert.   Sonata for Piano in C major, No. 15   (D.
      840)


529   "Remembrance"
      John Field.   Waltz for Piano in E major (sometimes,
      Nocturne No. 12)   (Hopkinson No. 51 A (e))

      The composer's title was "Sehnsuchts Walzer" but when
the publisher made an English edition of these waltzes the
E major one was called "Remembrance. "


530   "Reminiscence"
      Chopin.   Nocturne in C♯ minor, op. 27 no. 1   (Brown
      No. 49)

      This was published in the spring of 1830 together with
three mazurkas and entitled "Three Mazurkas and Adagio,
Juvenilia of Frédéric Chopin. "   In Poland the work is sometimes called the "Reminiscence" Nocturne because of the
self quotation from the second Concerto in F minor and
from the song "Zyczenie" [the wish].   At the head of the
Leitgeber's publication of the nocturne appear the words,
"Siostrze Ludwici dla wprawy,   nim się zabierze do mego
drugiego Koncertu" [for my sister Louise to play before
she practices my second concerto].   Chopin sent a copy of

the nocturne to his family from Vienna in 1830 written in
minute writing in one of his letters and may have indicated
that it was for his sister.    But the letter was destroyed in
the fire at the Zamojski Palace in 1863 and there is no
means of substantiating this inscription.


531    "Requiem"
       Howard Hanson.    Symphony No. 4

       This symphony was written to the memory of Dr. Han-
son's father.    The movements are written and named after
the parts of the Requiem service, Kyrie, Requiescat, Dies
Irae and Lux Aeterna.


532    "Requiem"
       Kabalevsky.    Symphony No. 3 (Choral)

       On December 26, 1933, Dmitri Kabalevsky completed
the composition of his choral Third Symphony, subtitled
"Requiem" and written as a symphonic song in memory of
Lenin.


533    "Restlessness"  (see "Songs Without Words")
       Mendelssohn.    Piece for Piano, op. 19 no. 5, in F#
          minor


534    "Resurrection" [Auferstehung]
       Mahler.    Symphony No. 2 in C minor

       During the years 1891 and 1893, when Mahler was
conductor at the Hamburg Opera and Hans von Bülow was
conductor at the Hamburg Philharmonic Orchestra, the two
were great friends.    When Mahler showed von Bülow
sketches of his Second Symphony, the latter was most help-
ful and encouraging.
       It was the final movement of this symphony that
was giving Mahler the most trouble, and ironically enough
it was not until he was at von Bülow's funeral rites and
heard the choir intone Klopstock's "Resurrection Ode" that
he got the idea which finally evolved into the impressive
last pages of his "Resurrection Symphony. "

535   "Retrospection"  (see "Songs Without Words")
      Mendelssohn.   Piece for Piano, op. 102 no. 3, in D
      major


536   "The Return"  (see "Songs Without Words")
      Mendelssohn.   Piece for Piano, op. 85 no. 5, in A
      major


537   "Reunion"
      Chopin.   Prelude, op. 28 no. 1, in C major   (Brown
      124)

      Each of the Op. 28 preludes of Chopin was given a
subtitle by Hans von Bülow, who wrote of this one:  "The
whole prélude expresses the joy of reconciliation after a
quarrel--in the stretto, indeed, this reaches extravagance,
only to regain tranquillity of happiness at the end.   This is
indicated by the final legatissimo chord of C" [Musician, xvi
(1911)].


538   "Reverie"  (see "Songs Without Words")
      Mendelssohn.   Piece for Piano, op. 85 no. 1, in F
      major


539   "Revolutionary"
      Chopin.   Etude for Piano, op. 10 no. 12, in C minor
      (Brown 67)

      When Chopin was in Stuttgart in 1831 he heard of the
capture of Warsaw by the Russians.   He was terribly upset
by the news and it is supposed to have inspired the wild
despair of the C minor Etude, nicknamed the "Revolutionary."  Sometimes, it is also referred to as "Fall of Warsaw."


540   "Rhenish"
      Schumann.   Symphony No. 3 in E♭ major, op. 97

      This symphony was inspired by a trip that the Schu-
manns had taken to Cologne.   Schumann was very much impressed with the physical beauties of the Rhineland and the
spiritual aura of the great cathedral.   He intended the

symphony as a picture of Rhenish life.

It is known that the solemn fourth movement with its organ-like motif was inspired by the recollection that Schumann had of the ceremony at the Cologne Cathedral at the installation of the Archbishop Geissel as cardinal. The Scherzo movement that follows has as its basic theme an old German drinking song.

"The Rhenish Symphony" was very dear to Schumann. When Carl Reinecke (July 1, 1851) made a four-hand piano arrangement of the symphony at Schumann's request, the composer wrote the following to him: "It is always important that a work which cost so much time and labor should be reproduced in the best possible manner."

541   "Rhodanienne"
      Milhaud.   Symphony No. 8 in D major

This symphony has been subtitled "Rhodanienne" by the composer because it is supposed to describe the Rhone River. The opening movement describes the birth of the river in the Rhone Glacier in Switzerland; the second, the Rhone crossing Lake Geneva; the third, the tumultuous river flowing towards southern France; and the last, the emptying of the river into the Mediterranean Sea.

542   "The Rider" [Der Reiter]
      Haydn.   String Quartet, op. 74 no. 3, in G minor
      (Hob. III, 73)

The first theme of the first movement of this quartet has a prancing rhythm that pervades the whole movement and it is because of this that it received its nickname.

543   "Riesen-Symphonie"   (see "Giant Symphony")
      Mahler.   Symphony No. 5 in C minor

544   "Il Riposo" [Repose]
      Vivaldi.   Concerto in E major for Violin and Strings
      (F. I, 4)

545   "Le Rire du Diable"
      Paganini.   Caprice for Violin No. 13 in B♭ major

There is a mocking descending theme in the Caprice
which has made some imaginative listeners think of a "devil's
chuckle" [rire du diable].


546   "A Rivulet"   (see "Songs Without Words")
      Mendelssohn.   Piece for Piano, op. 30 no. 5, in D
      major


547   "Rococo"
      Haydn.   Minuet No. 1 in C major; from set of 12 for
      Harpsichord   (Hob. IX, 8)

      Haydn wrote a great many minuets and allemandes for
balls and dances.   This is one of the set written in 1785,
published by Artaria and nicknamed "Rococo."


548   "Romantic"
      Howard Hanson.   Symphony No. 2

      Dr. Hanson writes the following about his Symphony
No. 2:   "Concerning my second Symphony, as the subtitle
implies, it represents for me definite and acknowledged em-
bracing of the romantic phrase.   I recognize, of course,
that romanticism is at the present time the poor stepchild,
without the social standing of her older sister, neoclassi-
cism....   My aim, in this symphony, has been to create a
work young in spirit, romantic in temperament, and simple
and direct in expression. "


549   "Romantic"   (see "The Song of the Night")
      Mahler.   Symphony No. 7 in E minor


550   "Romantic Symphony"
      Bruckner.   Symphony No. 4 in E♭ major

      According to Gabriel Engel, Bruckner wrote this sym-
phony in the village of Mondsee, a beautiful spot in the
Austrian Alps.   His own thoughts while writing the work
help to understand his subtitle:   "A citadel of the Middle
Ages...   Daybreak...   Reveille is sounded from the tower
...   The gates open...   Knights on proud chargers leap
forth...   The magic of nature surrounds them" [The Symphonies, p. 33].

551  "Romantica"
     Carlos Chávez.   Symphony No. 4

     The Symphony No. 4 was commissioned by the Louis-
ville Orchestra, and at the first performance it was called
a "Short Symphony. " However, the composer decided to
give it the subtitle "Romantica" instead, as an indication of
the very definite lyrical character of the work.


552  "Rondo Elégante"
     Chopin.   Introduction and Rondo for Piano in E♭ major,
        op. 16   (Brown 76)


553  "The Row in Vienna"  (see "The Frog")
     Haydn.  String Quartet, op. 50 no. 6, in D major
       (Hob. III, 49)


554  "La Roxolane"
     Haydn.  Symphony No. 63 in C major   (Hob. I, 63)

     The history of this symphony is very involved.  It is
thought that the reason for the nickname is the fact that the
French folk song "La Roxolane" is used as a theme for
variations in the Allegretto movement.


555  "The Royal Fireworks Music"
     Handel.   Suite in D major for Orchestra

     To celebrate the signing of the peace at Aix La Chap-
elle in October 1748, the King ordered great festivities with
fireworks and music.   Handel was sent for and instructed to
prepare music.   An Italian, Chevalier Servandoni, was to
supervise the erection, in London's Green Park, of a structure for a gigantic display of fireworks.   When this "ma-
chine, " a pseudo-Doric Temple, 410 feet long and 114 feet
high, was completed on April 26, 1749, it displayed the
arms of the Duke of Montagu, who was in charge of the
festivities, as well as figures of Greek Gods, a bas-relief
of George II and a pole rising about 200 feet and topped by
a huge symbol of the sun.
     Handel wrote a suite consisting of Overture, Alle-
gro, Lentement, Bourree, Largo alla siciliana, Allegro and
two Minuets to be played by a tremendous band of 40

trumpets, 20 French horns, 16 hautboys, 12 side drums, flutes and fifes.

On April 21, 1749, the "Royal Fireworks Music" was rehearsed publicly in the Spring Gardens, Vaux Hall. It was reported that 12,000 people paid two shillings six pence each to attend the rehearsal. London Bridge was so crowded that is became impassable for three hours. As the orchestra finished the Overture, 101 brass cannons blazed forth the royal salute. The fireworks structure was outlined in fiery light and suddenly the fireworks had become uncontrollable. The huge sun atop its 200 feet pole burst into flame, then part of the structure caught fire. There was pandemonium and many people were injured, two of them mortally.

The only success that had come of all this celebration was Handel's music. In May of the same year "The Royal Fireworks Music" was performed in the presence of the King for a large benefit concert for the Foundling Hospital. The King was delighted with the music, as have musicians all over the world been ever since.


556 "Russian"
Anton Rubinstein. Symphony No. 5 in G minor

The Symphony No. 5 is composed exclusively on Russian melodies, hence its nickname. In the Allegro movement there is a characteristic Russian Dance performed on wooden instruments in a very spirited manner.


557 "Russian Quartets"
Haydn. String Quartets, op. 33 (Hob. III, 37-42)

Haydn's string quartets, Op. 33, of 1781 (numbers 37 to 42 of Haydn's list) were dedicated to the Grand Duke Paul of Russia, and that is why they have been nicknamed "Russian." Sometimes they are called "Gli Scherzi" because this is the first time that scherzo is used instead of minuet. There is still another nickname, "Jungfernquartette." This was found on the title page of an old edition and is sometimes used.


558 "Rustic Wedding" [Ländliche Hochzeit]
Carl Goldmark. Symphony, op. 26 no. 1

This nickname was given to the symphony, or rather Suite, because of the labeling of the various movements which depict a wedding: I. "Wedding March"; II. "Bridal Song"; III. "Scherzo"; IV. "In the Garden"; V. "Finale." The question as to whether it really was a "rustic" wedding has been disputed because the fourth movement, "In the Garden," would not really fit. Peasants did not have gardens; that was quite a mark of social distinction.

559   "St. Anne's Fugue"
      J. S. Bach.   Fugue for Organ in E♭ major   (BWV
      552)

This name early became associated with the fugue in England, because of the similarity of the first subject with the familiar hymn tune by Dr. William Croft, called "St. Anne." Croft was the organist of St. Anne's Church, Soho, in London. The tune is found in many Protestant hymn books with the words, "O God, our help in ages past."

560   "St. Anthony"
      Haydn.   Feldpartita in B♭ major   (Hob. II, 46)

There are six Feldpartiten written by Haydn in the 1780's for the military band of Prince Esterházy. This one in B♭ major, scored for two oboes, two horns, three bassoons and B♭ "Serpent" (an obsolete bass cornet in the form of a snake), is the most important one. It has four movements; it is from the second movement, based on the "Chorale St. Antoni"--the old Austrian pilgrim's song--that the subtitle has had its origin.
      When Pohl showed a copy of this partita to his friend Johannes Brahms, the latter immediately copied the second movement in his notebook. Brahms used it as a theme for his "Variations on a Theme by Haydn," Op. 56, which he wrote during the summer of 1873.

561   "St. Bernardus of Offida Mass" (see "Holy Mass")
      Haydn.   Mass in B♭ major   (Hob. XXII, 10)

562   "Saint Cecilia Mass"   (see "Cantata Mass")
      Haydn.   Mass in C major   (Hob. XXII, 5)

563   "St. Joseph Mass"  (see "Nicolaimesse")
      Haydn.   Mass in G major  (Hob. XXII, 6)


564   "The Santa Fe Trail"
      Harl McDonald.  Symphony No. 1

      This symphony has been so subtitled because it reflects
the influence of McDonald's boyhood surroundings in the
Southwest.   McDonald says "My purpose in this work is to
recreate in tone something of the spirit and experiences of
these pioneers. "  In three movements:  I.  "The Explorers";
II.  "The Spanish Settlements"; III.  "The Wagon Trains of
the Pioneers. "  [From Philadelphia Orchestra program
notes, 1971-1972, p. 18.]


565   "The Saucy Maid" [Das kecke Beserl]
      Bruckner.  Symphony No. 1 in C minor

      Gabriel Engel [Symphonies of A. Bruckner, p. 5] ex-
plains that the carefree and skipping nature of the opening
theme of this symphony caused Bruckner to give it its nickname.   In later years, when Bruckner was pressed for an
explanation of the rash nature of this music, he merely
said with a sigh, "I was head over heels in love in those
days. "


566   "A Scene on the Place de Notre Dame de Paris"
      Chopin.   Prelude, op. 28 no. 17, in A♭ major (Brown
        100, no. 17)

      Each of the Op. 28 preludes of Chopin was given a
subtitle by Hans von Bülow.  He describes this one in the
following manner:  "A rendezvous by moonlight, interrupted
by the striking of the clocks in the churches near by.   One
can hear the mysterious whispers of an enamored couple at
the open window; at first subdued, then growing louder and
louder until they break into an outburst of passion (ff passage, A flat).   Again soft but rising to another climax at E
flat, an embrace (repetition of the chord of E flat) suddenly
followed by the first stroke of the clock.   The lovers
aroused from their ecstasy fall again to whispering.   The
clock strikes, they still whisper; the clock continues to
strike [until it] has given eleven strokes, then one last sigh
thrills the air" [Musician, xvi (1911)].

567   "Gli Scherzi"   (see "The Russian Quartets")
      Haydn.   Quartet, op. 33   (Hob. III, 37-42)


568   "Schöpfungsmesse"   (see "Creation Mass")
      Haydn.   Mass in B♭ major   (Hob. XXII, 13)


569   "The Schoolmaster"
      Haydn.  Symphony No. 55 in E♭ major   (Hob. I, 55)

The almost didactic character of the second movement
of the E♭ major Symphony is supposed to have given it its
nickname.   Another unusual thing in this workmanlike but
not too inspiring Symphony is the two sets of Variations,
one is the slow movement and another in the Finale.


570   "Scotch"
      Mendelssohn.   Symphony No. 3, op. 56, in A minor

In the summer of 1829 Mendelssohn visited Edinburgh
and rarely was a journey left with such poetic impressions
as this one.   A letter dated July 30, 1829, written by Mendelssohn, has the following:  "I believe I found today in that
old chapel the beginning of my 'Scotch Symphony'. "
      The first movement has been said to describe the
sombre impressions made upon the composer by his visit
to Holyrood.   The second is a picture of pastoral nature,
and the third, a revery in which the composer mediates
upon the ancient state and grandeur of the country.   In the
last movement, "the romantic sentiment disappears and
sometimes this is called the gathering of the clans. "


571   "Scotch Sonata" [Sonate Ecossaise]
      Mendelssohn.   Fantasie for Piano in F♯ minor, op. 28

The Fantasie in F♯ minor, often called "Sonate Ecossaise" by Mendelssohn, was supposed to have been composed
in 1833.   However, this is probably wrong because Mendelssohn writes of playing it for Goethe in 1830.   It was in the
summer of 1829 that Mendelssohn visited Edinburgh and it
can well be that the "Scotch Sonata" dates from that period,
as does the "Scotch Symphony. "

572  "A Sea Symphony"
     Vaughan Williams.    Symphony No. 1 for Chorus and
     Orchestra

     This is a choral orchestral work based on poems of
Walt Whitman.  The subtitles of the four movements inten-
sify the subtitle of the symphony: I. "A Song for All Seas,
All Ships"; II. 'On the Beach at Night Alone"; III. "The
Waves"; IV. "The Explorers. "

573  "The Seasons" [Die Jahreszeiten]
     Louis Spohr.    Symphony No. 9 in B minor, op. 143

     Spohr gave this subtitle to his Ninth Symphony, in
which he tried to depict the four seasons of the year.  He
divided the work into two grand themes, with the designa-
tions, Part I: Winter, transition to Spring, Spring; and
Part II: Summer, transition to Autumn, Autumn.

574  "Sechsviertel Messe"  (see "Six-Four Time Mass")
     Haydn.  Mass in G major (Nicolaimesse)  (Hob. XXII,
     6)

575  "Serenade"  (see "Songs Without Words")
     Mendelssohn.    Piece for Piano, op. 67 no. 6, in E
     major

576  "Serenade Quartet"
     Romanus Hoffstetter; attrib to Haydn.    String Quartet
     in F major, op. 3 no. 5  (Hob. III, 17)

     The slow movement of this quartet has long been popu-
lar under the name "Serenade," and the whole quartet has
been known under that title.  It is played by the first violin
in a singing fashion, to the accompaniment of the other
strings, which are plucked.  It has been published in many
transcriptions, under a variety of titles.  The six quartets
long ascribed to Haydn and published as his Op. 3 are,
however, the work of Romanus Hoffstetter, as explained in
articles by Tyson and Landon ["Who Composed Haydn's Op.
3?" Musical Times, 105 (1964), pp. 506-7] and by Somfai
["Zur Echtheitsfrage des Haydnschen 'Opus 3'," Haydn Year-
book, 3 (1965), pp. 153-63].

577   "Serenata Notturna"
      Mozart.   Serenade No. 6 in D major   (K. 239)

This serenade was written in Salzburg in January 1776,
but the exact occasion for the piece in not known.   Alfred
Einstein suggests that the two interpolations which occur
during the final Rondo are references to local tunes familiar to the Salzburgers and that, if we could but identify them,
they might tell us something of the work's purpose.   Be
that as it may, the Serenata speaks for itself, displaying
the wonderful ease of Mozart's imagination and a rather sly
side of his humor.

578   "Seven Rituals of Music"
      Henry Cowell.   Symphony No. 11

Virgil Thomson's record jacket notes on the Columbia
recording of this work tell us that Cowell used this subtitle
because in the seven movements of the symphony he tried
to depict the seven different rituals in the life of man from
birth to death.
     First movement--music for a child asleep; Second--
an Allegro describing the ritual of work, with some pro-
phetic hints of war; Third--a song for the ritual of love
with premonition of magic; Fourth--music for ritual of
dance and play with some reminiscences of music for work;
Fifth--the ritual of magic with some reference to the music
of the third movement, that of love; Sixth--for the ritual of
dance but also some hint of war, and refers back to man's
work; Seventh movement--the introduction to the last movement is a fugal exposition of themes of the preceding six
movements, then leading into music for the ritual of death
which begins as a lament and grows in intensity until the
end of the symphony.

579   "Shepherd Boy Etude"   (see "Aeolian Harp")
      Chopin.   Etude for Piano, op. 25 no. 1, in A♭ major
      (Brown 104)

580   "The Shepherd's Complaint"   (see "Songs Without
      Words")
      Mendelssohn.   Piece for Piano, op. 67 no. 5, in B
      minor

581   "Short G Minor"
      J. S. Bach.   Fugue for Organ in G minor   (BWV 578)

      The Fugue in G minor, labeled the "Short G Minor,"
was written in the master's first Weimar period and is
another example of his youthful spirits.   The music is tuneful, delightful and rhythmic.


582   "The Siege of Belgrade"   (see "The Battle")
      Mozart.   Contretanz for Orchestra   (K. 535)


583   "Sighing Wind"   (see "Songs Without Words")
      Mendelssohn.   Piece for Piano, op. 102 no. 4, in G
      minor


584   "Sinfonía de Antigona"
      Carlos Chávez.   Symphony No. 1

      The composer has endorsed the following notes by Her-
bert Weinstock, concerning his Sinfonía de Antigona:
      "In 1932 Carlos Chávez composed incidental music
for a staged performance in Mexico City of Jean Cocteau's
contraction of The Antigone of Sophocles.   From that incidental music he later drew the basic materials for the one
movement, 'Sinfonía de Antigona,' now listed as Symphony
No. 1.   The Orquesta Sinfónica de Mexico, with Chávez
conducting, played the premiere of the symphony on December 15, 1933.   At that time a program note prepared with
the composer's assistance read, "Inspired by the feelings
prevalent in the Greek tragedy, the Sinfonía Antigona, nevertheless, is not directly related to scenes in the drama.   It
is a symphony, not a symphonic poem:   The music has no
literary program.   Antigone, her exaltation and rebellion,
her heroism and martyrdom; these are expressed by the
entire symphony, not by its successive sections.   The atmosphere of intense tragedy is established in the first
measures and persists throughout, its expressive power re-
siding principally in the simplicity and sobriety of the musical materials employed.   The score breathes a certain ar-
chaic quality because of the use of rhythmic, harmonic and
melodic elements essential to ancient Greek music; the
themes are all modal, and the harmony is in fourth and
fifths, thirds having been avoided because the Greek musical
system treated them as dissonant. "

585   "Sinfonìa Espansiva"
      Carl Nielsen.   Symphony No. 3, op. 24

      The subtitle is not meant to be taken programmatically,
nor is the work unduly long.   "Espansiva" simply refers to
the growth of the mind and spirit and the widening of life's
horizons.


586   "Sinfonía India" [(American) Indian Symphony]
      Carlos Chávez.   Symphony No. 2

      The composer says that he has considered "India" [re-
ferring to North America] as a descriptive adjective or better yet as a subtitle.   He endorsed the following notes of
Herbert Weinstock:   "Carlos Chávez composed the 'Sinfonía
India' in New York during the winter of 1935-1936 and he
conducted its world premiere during a concert broadcast by
the Columbia Symphony Orchestra on January 23, 1936.
This is a true one movement Symphony based on an altera-
tion of the classical sonata-symphony pattern.   It is unusual
among Chávez's works in that it quotes true Indian melodies,
use being made of themes collected among the Seris of
Sonora, the Hiucholes of Nayarit and the Yaquis of Sonora.... "


587   "Sinfonia Sacra" [sacred symphony]
      Howard Hanson.   Symphony No. 5

      Dr. Hanson composed this symphony, which he subti-
tled, for the Philadelphia Orchestra at Eugene Ormandy's
invitation.   The composer has written the following notes
concerning his work:   "The 'Sinfonia Sacra' does not attempt
programmatically to tell the story of the first Easter but
does attempt to evoke some of the atmosphere of tragedy
and triumph, mysticism and affirmation of the story which
is the essential symbol of the Christian faith.... "


588   "Sinfonìa Semplice" [simple symphony]
      Carl Nielsen.   Symphony No. 6

      In a letter to his daughter Nielsen wrote that he was
beginning a Sixth Symphony which was to be of "completely
idyllic character. "   He said that he intended to write with
"the same simple enjoyment of pure sounds as the old a
cappella composers, " and hence the subtitle.

589 "Singulière" [singular; peculiar]
Franz Berwald. Symphony No. 5 in C major

In this symphony Berwald, who lived from 1796-1863,
showed himself to be a composer far ahead of his time. It
is because of his great experimentation in form that the
subtitle is most appropriate.


590 "Sintram"
G. T. Strong. Second Symphony op. 50

The subtitle is based upon the romance of that name
by the German Romantic writer Friedrich Heinrich Karl de
la Motte Fouqué and on Dürer's famous print, "Ritter Tod
und Teufel. "


591 "Six-Four Time Mass" [Sechsviertel Messe]
Joseph Haydn. Mass in G (Nicolaimesse) (Hob. XXII,
6)

Haydn was supposed to have nicknamed this particular
mass himself, the reason for it most likely being the pastoral character of the opening Kyrie which is written in
six-four time. Also known by other names. (see no. 441)


592 "Skittle Ground Trio" [Kegelstatt Trio]
Mozart. Trio for Piano, Clarinet and Viola (K. 498)

This trio was supposed to have received its nickname
from the fact that Mozart composed it during a game of
skittles (ninepins). Burk, in his Mozart and His Music,
says the following:
"Mozart wrote this trio for his pupil Francisca von
Jacquin. She would have played the piano part, Mozart the
viola and Stadler the clarinet. The later title, 'Kegelstatt
Trio,' came from the unlikely story that he composed it during a game of ninepins. The character of the music implies anything but haste--rather loving care in the combined
treatment of the three instruments... " [p. 403].


593 "Le Soir" (see "Le Matin, le Midi et le Soir")
Haydn. Symphony No. 8 in G major (Hob. I, 8)

594   "Le Soir et la Tempesta"
      Haydn.   Symphony No. 8 in G major   (Hob. I, 8)

This curious polyglot nickname was supposed to have
been given to the symphony by Haydn himself.   It is the
last of the trilogy of symphonies, "Le Matin, le Midi et Le
Soir. "


595   "Sonata Fantasy"
      Scriabin.   Sonata No. 2 in G minor, op. 19

This was subtitled by the composer.   His program
notes in the first edition say the following:
      "The second sonata reflects the influence of the sea.
The first movement represents a warm quiet night on a sea-
shore.   The development section is the dark agitation of the
deep, deep, ocean.   The E major middle section shows
caressing moonlight on the water coming after the first darkness of night.   The second movement represents the vast
expanse of the ocean when it is stormy and agitated" [from
Faubion Bowers, Scriabin, v. I, p. 226].


596   "Sonate Ecossaise"   (see "Scotch Sonata")
      Mendelssohn.   Fantasie for Piano in F♯ minor, op. 28


597   "The Song of a Great City"
      Delius.   Paris Nocturne for Orchestra

Delius subtitled this nocturne himself and wrote the
following about it:   "It is a nocturne and describes my impressions of night and early dawn with its peculiar street
cries and Pan's goatherd.   These cries are very characteristic of Paris and the piece begins and closes with them. "


598   "The Song of the Night"
      Karl Szymanowski.   Symphony No. 3, op. 27

The subtitle comes from the fact that the tenor solo in
the symphony is written to a poem by the 13th-century Per-
sian mystic, Jalal al-din Rumi, called "The Song of the
Night":   "Oh, do not sleep, friend, through the night. /
You a soul, while we are suff'ring through this night. /
Such quiet, others sleep .../ I and God alone together in

this night!/ What a roar!/ Joy arises,/ Truth with gleaming wing is shining, in this night! " [from Philadelphia Orchestra program notes, April 13, 1973, p. 18].


599    "Song of the Night"
       Mahler.   Symphony No. 7 in E minor

       The second and fourth movements of this symphony
have been labeled "Nachtmusiken" [nocturnes] by Mahler and
the nickname "Song of the Night" was derived from these.
The movements are romantic in character and sometimes
they are played in concerts as separate pieces.   The European premiere of this work, in its entirety, took place in
Prague, September 1908, and was conducted by Mahler.


600    "Song of the Traveller"  (see "Songs Without Words")
       Mendelssohn.   Piece for Piano, op. 85 no. 6, in B♭
          major


601    "Songs Without Words" [Lieder ohne Worte]
       Mendelssohn.   48 Pieces for the Piano

       Over a long period of years Mendelssohn wrote eight
sets of six short piano pieces each, with the overall title,
Lieder ohne Worte [songs without words].   Only a few of
these 48 pieces were given individual titles by the compos-
er--such as the three "Venetian Boat Songs," in G minor,
F♯ minor, and A minor [see entries 698-700].
       However, the well-known 19th-century pianist and
composer, Stephen Heller, supplied French titles for all the
others; these have been translated from French into English
in an edition of Songs Without Words published by the Hatch
Music Company in Philadelphia in 1898.   In 1918 a slightly
revised edition of this work, still using the Heller subtitles,
but with additional notes by the 20th-century pianist, Marguerite Long, was published in Paris by Senart.   However,
Marguerite Long only attributes 42 subtitles to Heller and
these are given in the original French.


602    "Sopra la Lontananza d'un Fratello Diletto"  (see "On
          the Departure of a Beloved Brother")
       J. S. Bach.   Capriccio for Piano in B♭ major  (BWV
          992)

603   "The Sorrowful Soul"  (see "Songs Without Words")
      Mendelssohn.   Piece for Piano, op. 53 no. 4, in F
      major


604   "Il Sospetto" [Suspicion]
      Vivaldi.   Concerto in C minor for Violin, Strings and
      Cembalo  (F. I, 2)


605   "Soul States"  (see "Etats d'Ame")
      Scriabin.   Sonata No. 3, op. 23, in F♯ major


606   "Souvenir d'Andalousie" [memories of Andalusia]
      Chopin.   Boléro for Piano, op. 19   (Brown 81)


607   "Souvenir de Florence" [memories of Florence]
      Tchaikovsky.   Sextet for Strings, op. 70, in D minor

      Tchaikovsky wrote the Sextet in D minor after a trip
to Italy in 1890.   It is written in one of the composer's rare
veins of happiness, serenity and pleasant memories of
Florence.   It was published in 1892 with this subtitle.


608   "Souvenir de la Pologne" [memories of Poland]
      Chopin.   51 Mazurkas for Piano

      Chopin's English publisher, Wessel, in the first Eng-
lish edition of the Complete Works, gave unauthorized names
to many of the compositions.   The 11 sets of mazurkas
were all given this title.


609   "Souvenir de Paganini"
      Chopin.   Variations in A major for Piano
      (Brown 37)

      Brown [Thematic Catalogue, p. 17] tells us that the
theme of these variations is the Venetian air "Le Carnaval
de Venise," used by Paganini himself as the basis of variations in his Op. 10.   Ludwig Bronarski suggested that
Paganini may have played this Op. 10 during his visit to
Warsaw May 23 to July 19, 1829, and that Chopin heard his
playing of it and was inspired to write these variations for
piano.

610   "Sparrows' Mass" [Spatzenmesse]
      Mozart.  Mass in C major  (K. 220)

      This mass was composed in Munich during Mozart's
preparation for his opera, La Finta Giardiniera.  It was
hardly composed for Munich; much rather for Salzburg, because Mozart would not have tried to impress a strange
community with one of his most elementary works.
      According to Einstein [Mozart, p. 336], the mass
is nicknamed "Sparrows' Mass," in the jargon of South
German Church musicians, because of the accompanying
figure of the violins in the Credo.


611   "The Spaur Mass"
      Mozart.  Mass in C major  (K. 258)

      In a letter that Mozart's father wrote on May 28,
1788, he refers to this mass as "The Spaur Mass."  It
was probably written for the consecration of Friedrich
Franz Joseph, Count von Spaur (later dean of the cathedral
in Salzburg), a ceremony in which the Archbishop took part.


612   "Spinning Song"  (see "Songs Without Words")
      Mendelssohn.  Piece for Piano, op. 67 no. 4, in C
      major

      This piece has always been known by its nickname
"Spinning Song," supposedly given to it by the pianist and
composer, Stephen Heller.  Ernest Hutcheson, in his book,
The Literature of The Piano [p. 145], says that in his
Australian boyhood it was also known under the pretty title
of "The Bee's Wedding."


613   "Spitzweg"
      Ernst Toch.  Serenade in G major, op. 25

      The composer writes the following about his composi-
tion:  "Spitzweg is the name of a German nineteenth century
painter with great charm and sense of humor.  The Serenade which I have nicknamed after him has been inspired by
one of his paintings entitled 'Serenade' accidentally coming
into my hands during World War I."


614   "Spring"
      J. K. Paine.  Symphony No. 2 in A major

615  "Spring Quintet" [Frühlings Quintett]
     Brahms.   String Quintet, op. 88, in F major

In the spring of 1882 Brahms wrote this work, which
became popularly known as the "Spring Quintet. "  The music
is ingratiating, warm, tuneful, joyous and as beautiful as a
spring day.


616  "Spring Sonata" [Der Frühling]
     Beethoven.   Sonata for Violin and Piano, op. 24, in F
     major

This sonata was composed in 1800 and published in
1801.   It is delightfully bright and cheerful and full of even,
rippling figures.   The nickname was given to it in Germany
and is most appropriate.


617  "Spring Song" [Frühlingslied]  (see "Songs Without
     Words")
     Mendelssohn.   Piece for Piano, op. 62 no. 6, in A
     major

In Germany this joyous lyrical little piece has always
been known as "Frühlingslied. "  However, when Mendelssohn was composing the piece he was visiting his English
friends, the Beneckes, who lived at Denmark Hill near
Camberwell Green and because of this it is known in England by the nickname, "Camberwell Green. "


618  "Spring Symphony" [Der Frühling]
     Schumann.   Symphony, op. 38 no. 1, in B♭ major

Schumann himself spoke of this as "Spring Symphony, "
even though it is not called so in the score.   In a letter to
Spohr (November 23, 1842) Schumann wrote, "I composed
the symphony, if I may so, under the impulse of that vernal
ardor, which sways men, even at a most advanced age. "
He also wrote to William Taubert (January 10, 1843) who
was to conduct this symphony in Berlin.   "Could you imbue
your orchestra with something of the springtime mood,
which I had particularly in mind when I wrote the Symphony
in February, 1841? "  He goes on in more detail, "The
trumpet call at the entrance, I should like to have sound as
if it came from on high like an awakening summons.   By

what follows, I might then suggest how, on every side, it
begins to grow green.   Now perhaps a butterfly appears,
and by the Allegro how all springtime things burst forth. "


619    "Stadler Quintet"
       Mozart.   Clarinet Quintet in A major   (K. 581)

       Mozart wrote this quintet in 1789 for Anton Stadler,
an excellent clarinettist for whom Mozart also composed his
clarinet Concerto in A (K. 622).   The clarinet was Mozart's
special love and Stadler had his great esteem as a musician, friend and fellow Mason.


620    "The Stalingrad Sonata"
       Prokofiev.   Sonata No. 7 in B♭ major, op. 83

       Milton Cross and David Ewen [Encyclopedia of the
Great Composers, v. II, p. 578] explain that this sonata
was written in 1942 during the heroic stand and final victory of the Red Army in Stalingrad.   Its power and grandeur
reflect the heroism that turned the tide of Stalingrad.   With
this sonata, Serge Prokofiev won the Stalin Prize for the
first time.


621    "La Steinquerque"
       Couperin.   Sonata in G major for Two Violins

       According to Wilfred Mellers [François Couperin, p.
104], the composer wrote this sonata for two violins in
honor of the victory at Steinquerque and that is the reason
for the subtitle.   It is an Italianized version of Lully's battle music.   A work in a grand manner befitting a ceremonial occasion.


622    "The Storm"
       Chopin.   Prelude, op. 28 no. 24, in D minor  (Brown
          107, no. 24)


       Each of the Op. 28 preludes of Chopin was given a
subtitle by Hans von Bülow, whose commentary on this one
is, "The left hand brings the storm hither; the right hand
declaims a dramatic motive.   A flash suddenly illuminates
the darkness (right hand scale)--a tree is shattered; it can
be seen by the glare of the lightning.   The storm increases

in fury; continuous flashes now fill the air--yet no rain! A
weird rumble is heard in the distance (C minor); it comes
nearer (D flat major).   Suddenly a wild blaze lights up the
whole scene.   It storms more and more furiously, until at
last mighty cloud-burst (descending chromatic scale) brings
down a deluge (the left hand seeks refuge on A where it
makes a pedal point).   The tempest continues; trees are
uprooted, the thunder crashes--a blinding flash bearing de-
struction in its wake ends the piece with dramatic emphasis" [Musician, xvi (1911)].


623   "Storm Quintet"
      Beethoven.   Quintet in C major, op. 29 (two violins,
         two violas, cello)

      It is in the final movement of this quintet that the
nickname has its origin.   The rapid flutter of repeated
notes extended into a stormy agitation of 16th notes, together with lightning scales darting from the first violin and
later alternating with the cello, give the illusion of a storm.


624   "Storm Rondo"
      Daniel Steibelt.   Third movt, Concerto No. 3, in E
         major for Piano

      This movement, subtitled "Storm Rondo" by Steibelt,
had enormous popularity.   It was probably performed for
the first time at the Salomon Concerts in London on March
19, 1798 [from Grove's Dictionary, 3d. ed., v. V, p. 129].


625   "Strassburg Concerto"
      Mozart.   Concerto for Violin No. 4 in D major   (K.
         218)

      The Fourth Concerto is always referred to in Mozart's
letters as his "Strassburg Concerto. " This is probably so
because in the last movement there is a theme reminiscent
of a Strassburg Dance.
      In a letter Leopold Mozart wrote to his son, dated
Salzburg, October 5, 1777, there is this interesting bit:
"On Saturday I was at the play.   As there was a French
epilogue, Brunetti had to play a concerto while the actors
were changing dresses, and he played your Strassburg Concerto most excellently" [from Letters, transl. by Emily
Anderson, V. I, p. 433].

626    "Street Song" [Gassenhauer]
       Beethoven.   Trio for Clarinet, Cello and Piano, op.
       11

    In October 1798 a trio for clarinet, cello and piano,
Op. 11, was announced by Beethoven's publisher, Mollo, as
"wholly new. "  The last movement consists of a series of
ten variations on the theme of a trio from a contemporary
opera by Weigl, L'Amor Marinaro.  It begins, "Pria ch'io
l'impegno. "  Beethoven took the theme at the request of an
obscure clarinet player for whom he wrote the trio, and
the nickname is probably derived from this song.


627    "Suffocation"
       Chopin.   Prelude, op. 28 no. 4, in E minor   (Brown
       123, no. 4)

    According to Hans von Bülow, who gave subtitles to
each of Chopin's Op. 28 preludes, the following reflects the
composer's feelings and intention with the utmost accuracy:
"Here is pictured one of the paroxysms to which Chopin
was subject on account of his weak chest.   In the left hand
we hear his heavy breathing, in the right hand the tones of
suffering wrung from his breast.   At the twelfth measure
he seeks relief by turning on the other side; but his oppression increases momentarily.   At the stretto he groans, his
pulse redoubles its beat, he is near death; but toward the
end he breathes more quietly (the chords must be breathed
rather then played).   His heart throbs grow slower and
fainter; at the chord resting on B flat (third measure from
the end) they suddenly cease for a moment.   Four eighth
notes must be counted to every half note so that these
beats, though not audible, may yet be felt.   The final
chords show that he sleeps" [Musician, xvi (1911)].


628    "Suicide"
       Chopin.  Prelude, op. 28 no. 18, in F minor   (Brown
       107, no. 18)

    Hans von Bülow gave each of Chopin's Op. 28 preludes
a subtitle.   Of this one he commented, "An unhappy creature
in a state of frenzy mounts a height.   As he climbs higher
and higher his brain turns at the sight of the depth below
him, but he still continues climbing.   He reaches the tower
at the top (eighth notes), one step, then another; now there

are but four small projections.   These surmounted, he
springs into the yawning abyss below, his body is dashed
to pieces (double trill with following figure),--horror and
consternation overwhelm the bystanders.   The short drama
closes with two chords" [Musician, xvi (1911)].


629   "Sun Quartets"
      Haydn,   Six Quartets, op. 20, for Strings:  1.  E♭
      major; 2.  C major; 3.  G minor; 4.  D major; 5.  F
      minor; 6.  A major   (Hob. III, 31-36)

      According to Karl Geiringer, the date of composition
of these so called "Sun Quartets" is usually given incorrectly.   The autograph copy, formerly in the possession of
Johannese Brahms, but bequeathed by him to the Society of
Friends of Music in Vienna, gives the date as 1772.   The
nickname for the six quartets supposedly originated because
of the lovely symbol of the rising sun which had been en-
graved on the title page of an old edition.


630   "Sunday"
      Chopin.   Prelude, op. 28 no. 21, in B♭ major
      (Brown 123, no. 21)

      Each of Chopin's Op. 28 preludes was given a subtitle
by Hans von Bülow.   This one he described as follows.
"The people are going to church:  women with prayerbooks
and carrying roses, followed by old men and children.   The
bells begin to chime (passage in G flat; the left hand very
legato, so that they may ring out sonorously), the air vi-
brates with their tones.   Mass is over, the people stream
out from the church (ff); toward the last a few scattered
ones, at the end one only.   After the last has gone one can
plainly hear the care-takers mount the steps of the church
and close the doors (in the two closing chords the C and B
flat of the middle voice are to be brought out distinctly"
[Musician, xvi (1911)].


631   "The Sunrise"
      Haydn.   String Quartet, op. 76 no. 4, in B♭ major
      (Hob. III, 78)

      The fourth quartet of the set of six, written in 1790,
is popularly known as "The Sunrise. "  It is in the first

movement that the nickname had its origin. The beautiful main theme, played by a violin, seems to soar above a rather dark accompaniment, giving the impression of a sunrise.

632 "Surprise Symphony"
Haydn. Symphony No. 94 in G major (Hob. I, 94)

A symphony as famous as the G major, "The Surprise," or, as it became known in Germany, "Mit dem Paukenschlag" [with the kettledrums], would naturally receive a great deal of comment. A well-known anecdote is attributed to Haydn's fondness for a joke. It seems that he had noticed that the English public kept at least one eye open during his Allegros and Scherzos, but, as he said, "slept peacefully during the slow movements." To remedy this, he suddenly, in a very quiet section of the second movement, when the strings playing alone had become very soft, had the whole orchestra, including the drums, play fortissimo. Everyone awoke with a start!
G. A. Griesinger has still another story: "I asked him once in jest if it were true that he wrote the Andante with the kettledrum beat in order to awaken the English public that had gone to sleep at his concert. 'No,' he answered me. 'Rather it was my wish to surprise the public with something new, and to make a debut in a brilliant manner, so as not to be outdone by my pupil, Pleyel, who at that time was engaged by an orchestra in London (in the year 1792) which had begun its concert series eight days before mine. The first Allegro of my Symphony was received with countless bravos, but the enthusiasm reached its highest point in the Andante with the kettledrum beat. Ancora, Ancora sounded from every throat and even Pleyel complimented me on my idea'" [Biographische Notizen über J. Haydn, p. 55].

633 "Swan Song" [Schwanengesang]
Haydn. String Quartet, op. 103, in B♭ major (Hob. III, 83)

In 1803 Haydn began his last string quartet, Op. 103 (No. 93 of Haydn's list). He wrote only two movements, an Andante grazioso and a Minuet. The quartet remained unfinished and was eventually published in 1806 with the nickname 'Swan Song."

At the end of the Minuet is a reproduction of the
visiting card which Haydn used during the last years of his
life.   On it was printed a quotation from the Master's favorite four part song, "Der Greis" [the old man], "Hin ist alle
meine Kraft; alt und schwach bin ich" [gone forever is my
strength; old and weak am I] [from Karl Geiringer, Haydn,
p. 281].


634   "Sweet Remembrance" (see "Songs Without Words")
      Mendelssohn.   Piece for Piano, op. 19 no. 1, in E
      major


635   "Symphony for Fun"
      Don Gillis.   Symphony No. 5 1/2

      The composer called the symphony "No. 5 1/2" be-
cause it was written while marking time between the num-
bered symphonies 5 and 6.   And he then subtitled the work
"Symphony for Fun."   The movements are:   Perpetual Motion, Scherzophrenia, Spiritual, and Conclusion [from
Slonimsky, Music Since 1900, p. 599].


636   "Symphony 1933"
      Roy Harris.   Symphony No. 1

      This symphony was first performed from manuscript
by the Boston Symphony Orchestra, January 26, 1934.   Apparently Mr. Harris composed the work in 1933 and that is
the reason for his subtitle.   His notes merely explain what
he tried to do:
      "In the first movement I have tried to capture the
mood of adventure and physical exhuberance.   In the second,
of the pathos which seems to underlie all human existence.
In the third, the mood of a positive will to power and action" [from Nicolas Slonimsky, Music Since 1900, p. 372-3].


637   "Symphony No. 6"
      Bohuslav Martinu.   Fantaisies Symphoniques for Or-
      chestra

      Martinu began writing his symphony in New York in
1951.   Originally he called it the "New Fantastic Symphony."
It was only when he completed the work in Paris in 1953

that he changed its title in order not to repeat the name of
Berlioz's celebrated work.  On that occasion he gave it the
subtitle of "Symphony No. 6. "

638   "Symphony of a Thousand"
      Mahler.  Symphony No. 8 in E♭ major

The arrangements for the premiere of this symphony
were made by a Munich impresario, Emil Guttmann.  As a
publicity stunt, he used the slogan "Symphony of a Thousand. "  The reason for this probably originated in the fact
that Mahler used a great number of singers in the choruses.
The advertising for this performance was launched in such
a noisy manner that Mahler alluded to it as his "Barnum
and Bailey performance. "

639   "Symphony of Heavenly Lengths"  (see "The Great")
      Schubert.  Symphony No. 7 in C major  (D. 944)

640   "Symphony of Pauses"
      Bruckner.  Symphony No. 2 in C minor

It appears from letters that Bruckner, who in 1868 had
given up his position as organist of Linz Cathedral to take
up a professorship at the Vienna Conservatoire, felt obliged
to take the wishes of audiences into consideration when writing the Second Symphony.  It is certainly clear that he
strove to make his work more understandable, a fact indicated by the numerous pauses which it contains.  These
were intended to clarify the formal structure for the listeners and to bridge abrupt contrasts.  This caused the work
to receive its nickname.

641   "Symphony of the City"
      Carl Eppert.  Symphony No. 1

This symphony has four separate parts and each of
these has a subtitle.  As a whole the music depicts the
struggles, the pleasures and the various aspects of life in
the great American cities of today.  Part I, op. 50 (Allegro movt) "Traffic"; Part II, op. 51 (Andante movt) "City
Shadows"; Part III, op. 53 (Scherzo movt) "Speed"; and
Part IV, op. 55 (Romance) "City Nights. "

642   "Symphony of the Land"
Carl Eppert.   Symphony No. 3 in C minor, op. 67

It is actually the subtitles of the four movements which
suggest the reason this work is known as the "Symphony of
the Land":  I. "The Tillers"; II. "The Earth Borne"; III.
"Slow Winter"; and IV. "The Yield. "


643   "Symphony of the Summits"
Lazare Saminsky.   Symphony No. 2 in H-fri-dur [free
major mode on B]

Nicolas Slonimsky [Music Since 1900, p. 231] writes
"The second symphony by the Russian symphonist of the
Rimsky-Korsakov school, Lazare Saminsky, subtitled "Symphony of the Summits," in a tonality designated as H-fri-dur
(free major mode in B), [was] performed for the first time
by the Concertgebouw Orchestra in Amsterdam on November
16, 1922, Willem Mengelberg conducting. "


644   "Symphony with a Bell"
Khatchaturian.   Symphony No. 2

This symphony was subtitled by the Russian critic
Kubov.   He has written an analysis of this work which
points out the reasons for his choice.
"In the first movement there is an introduction consisting of two elements--a bell motive which shudders loudly
through the entire orchestra, and a theme for strings.  In
the third movement the music ends in a great climax with
the bell motive.   And in the fourth movement there is a
grand climax attained as the bell theme and the brass chorus
thunder out an idea symbolic of triumph" [David Ewen,
World of 20th-Century Music, p. 418].


645   "Talin"
Hovhaness.   Concerto for Viola and String Orchestra,
op. 93

Talin is the name of a magnificent ruined Christian
Armenian Cathedral of the seventh century.  The nickname
serves as a suggestive index to the essential religious nature of the composition.

646   "Tarentelle"   (see "Songs Without Words")
      Mendelssohn.   Piece for Piano, op. 102 no. 3, in C
      major

647   "The Tempest"
      Beethoven.   Sonata for Piano, op. 31 no. 2, in D
      minor

It is said that when Schindler asked Beethoven the
meaning of the D minor Sonata, Op. 31, No. 2, Beethoven
told him to read Shakespeare's The Tempest.
      Donald Francis Tovey, in his book, A Companion
to Beethoven's Pianoforte Sonatas [p. 128], has the following to say:  "With all the tragic power of its first movement, the D minor Sonata is, like Prospero, almost as far
beyond tragedy as it is beyond mere foul weather.  It will
do you no harm to think of Miranda at bars 31-38 of the
slow movement, but people who want to identify Ariel and
Caliban and the castaways, good and villainous, may as
well confine their attention to the exploits of the Scarlet
Pimpernel when the Eroica or the C Minor Symphony is
being played. "

648   "La Tempesta di Mare"
      Vivaldi.   Concerto in E♭ major for Violin and Strings;
      Concerto in F major for Flute, Strings and Organ;
      Concerto in F major for Flute, Oboe, Bassoon,
      Strings and Harpsichord  (F. I, 26; VI, 12; & XII,
      28)

Each work separately is known as "La Tempesta di
Mare. "

649   "Tempo di Ballo"
      Scarlatti.   Sonata for Piano  (L. 463, K. 430)

650   "Theresa Mass" [Theresienmesse]
      Haydn.   Mass No. 3 in B♭ major  (Hob. XXII, 12)

The Third Mass in B♭ major was composed in 1799.
There have been several conjectures as to whom it was
written for.  Schnerich thought that the mass was named after the singer, Therese Rosenbaum-Gassman, but this does

not seem very likely.  It is probably Empress Maria Theresa, the second wife of Emperor Francis II, whom Haydn
had in mind.  She was one of his patronesses and also a
very gifted singer.


651   "Theresienmesse"   (see "Theresa Mass")
      Haydn.   Mass No. 3 in B♭ major  (Hob. XXII, 12)


652   "Thesis"
      Henry Cowell.   Symphony No. 15

      This symphony was subtitled by the composer.  It is
really not a symphony because it is made up of brief movements, but actually a suite.  The movements are as follows:
Largo, Andante, Presto, Allegro and Allegro Moderato.


653   "Thou Art So Like a Flower"
      Chopin.   Prelude, op. 28 no. 3, in G major  (Brown
         107, no. 3)

      Hans von Bülow, in inventing names for all the Chopin
Op. 28 preludes, chose for this the first line of one of the
best-known poems in the German language, Heinrich Heine's
"Du bist wie eine Blume. "  These words actually do fit the
opening phrase in the right hand in measures three to six.
Von Bülow's commentary on this work follows:  "An angel
flits through the open window and hovering over a sleeping
child, whispers the words of Heine's poem.  One can plainly
hear (passage in C major) the words, 'Praying that God may
preserve thee. '  At the end th[e] angelic visitor flies away"
[Musician, xvi (1911)].


654   "Three Mysteries"
      Paul Creston.   Symphony No. 3, op. 48

      Creston says that he gave this subtitle to his symphony
because of the three movements, "The Nativity," "The
Crucifixion," and "The Resurrection. "  The work is based
on the life of Christ, and utilizes at least two Gregorian
themes in each movement, taken from the Catholic liturgy,
dealing with the particular period in the life of Christ.

655   "Thun"   (see "Meistersinger")
      Brahms.   Sonata for Violin and Piano, op. 100, in A
      major


656   "The Thunderstorm" [Das Donnerwetter]
      Mozart.   Contretanz for Orchestra   (K. 534)

   This Contretanz for Orchestra was so subtitled in the
original score.   It was also transcribed for the harpsichord
or piano by Mozart.


657   "Timber"
      Carl Eppert.   Symphony No. 4 in F major, op. 70

   The reason for the subtitle is that the symphony tries
to depict the story of the Birth, Life, Death and Glorification of the great trees.   First movement--"Story of Birth
of Trees"; second--"Life of Trees"; and third--"Death and
Glorification of Great Trees. "


658   "The Titan"
      Mahler.   Symphony No. 1 in D major

   This symphony was named after the novel of the same
name by the German Romantic author, Jean Paul Richter.
Mahler derived a program from the novel to explain his
symphony.   Actually, the book has little or nothing to do
with the symphony, because Mahler made up the program
after composing it.   He did this only to make the music
more appealing to an audience.


659   "Titans"
      William Russo.   Symphony No. 2 in C major

   The composer writes as to why he refers to his symphony No. 2 as "Titans": "I see man as potentially great--
even heroic--not as an ant, instinctually driven and power-
less in the world. "


660   "Toccata Study"
      Chopin.   Etude for Piano, op. 10 no. 7, in C major
         (Brown 68)

661 "Toccata 10"
    Scarlatti.  Sonata for Piano  (K. 85 & K. 82)

    According to Ralph Kirkpatrick [Domenico Scarlatti, p. 150], some of Scarlatti's earliest harpsichord music is to be found in a Portuguese manuscript (Coimbra manuscript 58). In this manuscript is a four-movement piece incorporating the Sonata K. 85 and 82. It is always referred to as "Toccata 10."

662 "Der Tod und das Mädchen"  (see "Death and The
    Maiden")
    Schubert.  String Quartet, op. 161, in D minor  (D.
    810)

663 "Tolling Bells"
    Chopin.  Prelude, op. 28 no. 6, in B minor  (Brown
    107, no. 6)

    Each of the Op. 28 preludes of Chopin was given a subtitle by Hans von Bülow. This one he described as follows: "The tolling motive in the right hand calls for no rubato, no feeling; it must express no compassion, no pity whatever. In the left hand the soul of the dying one appears to have left the body and to be wandering through infinite space until it reaches the path to eternity. At the next to the last measure the bell breaks off--then four strokes are heard trembling in the air" [Musician, xvi (1911)].

664 "Le Tombeau" [The Tomb]
    J. M. Leclair.  Sonata for Violin and Continuo in C
    minor

    It was given this nickname because of the sad style of the music.

665 "Torrent"
    Chopin.  Etude for Piano, op. 10 no. 4, in C♯ minor

666 "Tost Quartets"
    Haydn.  String Quartets, op. 54-55, 64  (Hob. III, 57-
    68)

The 12 string quartets, numbers 57 through 68, were
published during the years 1789-1790 and were dedicated to
Johann Tost, a violinist and merchant.    It is because of
this that they are known by the nickname "Tost Quartets."
      Karl Geiringer has the following interesting bit to
say about Tost:    "There seems to be some doubt about the
personality of this man.    Pohl (II. 373) mentions a violinist
of this name who was a member of the Esterházy Orchestra
from 1783 to 1789.    In 1789 he went to Paris and there he
carried out dubious transactions with some of Haydn's symphonies and string quartets.    About the later fate of this
man nothing is known.    However, in 1790 a second Johann
Tost, who was also a violinist, made his appearance in
Haydn's biography (Pohl II. 228).    In 1790 Johann Tost II
married a rich girl and became a respected cloth merchant.
He was the man to whom Haydn dedicated his twelve quartets.    The author feels inclined to share Larsen's assump-
tion that Tost I and Tost II were the same person.    It is
certainly surprising that we know nothing about the life of
Johann Tost I after 1790, and nothing about the life of Johann
Tost II before 1790" [A Creative Life, p. 254].


667    "Toy Symphony"
       Leopold Mozart; attrib to Haydn.    Symphony in C ma-
         jor   (Hob. II, 47)

      There have been conflicting stories concerning the ori-
gin of the "Toy Symphony."    Following are two of them:
      A traditional account is that Haydn purchased seven
toy instruments at a fair at Berchtesgaden.    He took them
to Esterháza and summoned his orchestra to an important
rehearsal.    When the men discovered that they were expected to play a new symphony on these toys (the only real
instruments in the score are two violins and a double bass),
they laughed so hard that they could scarcely play.    To make
the symphony even more amusing, the last of the three
movements is played three times, each time faster and
faster.
      H. C. Robbins Landon, in his book, The Symphonies
of Joseph Haydn [p. 45], says that in the Stams Monastery
(Tyrol) there is a curious MS. of the "Toy Symphony" ascribed to Rev. D. Edmundo Angerer, and entitled "Berch-
toldsgaden Musick."    (The MS. only is a further proof that
this work cannot possibly be by Haydn.)    He goes on to say
that Ernst Fritz Schmid has discovered a MS. by Leopold
Mozart in the Bavarian State Library of Munich, in which

the three movements of the "Toy Symphony" are included.
And Nicolas Slonimsky in his 1971 edition of Baker's
Biographical Dictionary of Musicians [p. 677] says: "Thus
the celebrated Toy Symphony appears not to be a work by
Haydn but by Leopold Mozart. "


668    "Tragic"
       Bruckner,   Symphony No. 5 in B♭ major

This symphony, nicknamed by Goellerich, Bruckner's
faithful biographer, has had several other nicknames attributed to it.   It has been called "Pizzicato Symphony" because plucked strings play an important part in it; "Church
of Faith Symphony" because of many choral passages; and
Bruckner himself called it "Fantastic. "
However, "Tragic" is the most fitting of them all
because Bruckner wrote it in the very midst of a long period of heart-breaking frustrations.   It was really a deep personal expression of a genius doomed to utter loneliness by
the scorn and neglect of a misunderstanding world.


669    "Tragic"
       Mahler.   Symphony No. 6 in A minor

After Mahler had written this gloomy composition,
known by its popular name "Tragic, " one of his friends,
shocked by the extreme bitterness which swayed this work,
asked him reproachfully "How could a man as kindhearted
as you, have written a Symphony so full of bitterness? "
Mahler replied "It is the sum of all the suffering I
have had to endure at the hands of life" [from Chord and
Discord, 1938, p. 32].


670    "Tragic"
       Schubert.   Symphony No. 4 in C minor   (D. 417)

The popular title of this symphony was given to the
work by Schubert, probably on the occasion of a later,
though unauthenticated, performance in the so-called "Gun-
delhof" under the direction of the violinist Otto Hatwig.
Schubert tried to emulate Beethoven in this symphony, but he was not very successful.   It is only in the
beautiful slow movement that Schubert really holds his own
and one feels its "tragic" mood.

671   "Tragic Landscape"
      Arnold Bax.   Winter Waters; Piece for Piano

      Perhaps the subtitle came to this piece because it
achieves a sinister atmosphere with a menacing ground bass
of four notes that continues throughout.


672   "Tragic Overture"
      Brahms.   Overture, op. 81, in D minor

      Brahms was unable to settle on a title for this over-
ture and he wrote his friend, Billroth: "In earlier days my
music failed to please me; now it is my titles too.   In the
end that sort of thing is vanity. "   Finally, "Tragic Overture" was used as a subtitle.
      Both Hamlet and Faust have been mentioned in con-
nection with this work; Brahms, however, did not leave a
clue as to the meaning of this music or of his intentions.
It is generally agreed that the Master had no definite tragic
figure in mind, but that only the universal and constant
emotion of tragedy is reflected here.


673   "Tragic Polonaise"
      Chopin.   Polonaise, op. 44, in F♯ minor   (Brown 135)

      James Huneker in his book, Chopin--The Man and His
Music, gives the following account of the nickname:   "It
starts with a roar in F♯ and finally a silence which marks
the cessation of an agitating nightmare.   A confession from
the dark depth of a self tortured soul" [p. 187].


674   "Tragica"
      MacDowell.   Sonata for Piano No. 1, op. 45, in G
      major

      It has been suggested that the memory of MacDowell's
grief over the death of his teacher, Raff, might have given
him the idea for the work with its popular title "Tragica. "
The composer does say that in the first three movements
he attempted to express tragic details and in the Finale he
wanted to heighten the darkness of tragedy by making it follow closely on the heels of triumph.

675    "Trauer-Symphonie" [Mourning or Funeral Symphony]
       Haydn.    Symphony No. 44 in E minor    (Hob. I, 44)

Haydn intended the symphony to be a lament on the death of a hero. It is said that he was so moved by the beautiful Adagio that he wanted it played at his own funeral service.

676    "Trauerwalzer" [Funeral Waltz]
       Schubert.    Waltz, op. 9 no. 2   (D. 365, No. 2)

Towards the end of 1829 Cappi and Diabelli published a number of dances of Schubert (Op. 9) under the title, "Original Dances for the Pianoforte." Among these is this No. 2, to which the publishers gave the popular nickname, "Trauerwalzer." This is rather comical because it is no more "funereal" than all the rest of the Op. 9.

677    "Triangle Concerto"
       Liszt.    Concerto for Piano No. 1 in E♭ major

The use of a triangle in the finale of the score of the E♭ major Concerto caused some discussion in Vienna, and the famous critic, Hanslick, nicknamed the work, "A Triangle Concerto" intending his remark to be a derogatory one.

678    "Trill Sonata"
       Scriabin.    Sonata No. 10, op. 70

Faubion Bowers, in his biography, Scriabin (v. II, p. 244), nicknamed this sonata. He writes the following: "Its harmonic symetry based on major thirds shrinking swiftly into minor thirds sets up a vortex of interior diminution constantly raised by trills and tremolos."

679    "Il Trillo del Diavolo"   (see "The Devil's Trill")
       Giuseppe Tartini.    Sonata for Violin in G minor

680    "Triumphal Chant"   (see "Songs Without Words")
         (sometimes, "Folk Song")
       Mendelssohn.    Piece for Piano, op. 53 no. 5, in A
         minor

681    "The Trout" [Die Forelle]
       Schubert.    Piano Quintet, op. 114, in A major    (D.
       667)

       In the summer of 1819, when Schubert was composing
his famous Quintet in A major for piano, violin, viola, cello
and bass, a friend suggested that he include in it variations
on his song, "Die Forelle." Schubert agreed and, between
the Scherzo and Finale, he inserted a set of six variations
on phrases from the song--hence the nickname.


682    "Trumpet Overture"
       Mendelssohn.    Overture, op. 101, in C major

       The so-called "Trumpet Overture" was composed in
1825. It is based on a simple theme vividly developed by
the wind instruments against a background of strings. It is
scored for two flutes, oboes, clarinets in C, horns in C,
trumpets in C, bassoons, three trombones and strings. The
origin of the nickname is a mystery, because the trumpets
actually do less than the horns.
       This piece seemed to have been a great favorite of
Mendelssohn. In November 1832 the composer was commissioned by the London Philharmonic Society to compose (for a
fee of 100 guineas) "a symphony, an overture and a vocal
piece." The symphony submitted was the "Italian"; the overture, "The Hebrides," but instead of writing the desired
vocal composition, Mendelssohn presented the Society with
another overture, "The Trumpet."


683    "Trumpet Sonata"
       Mozart.    Sonata for Piano in D major    (K. 576)

       This brilliant sonata, which Mozart wrote in 1789, is
sometimes known by the above nickname because of the fanfare-like character of its opening theme.


684    "Turkish"
       Mozart.    Concerto for Violin No. 5 in A major    (K.
       219)

       It is in the last movement of this concerto with its
humorous outbreak of sound and fury in "Turkish" style that
the nickname had its origin. According to Einstein, Mozart

borrowed the noisy tutti in A minor of this "Turkish" inter-
lude from himself; it had originally occurred in the ballet
Le Gelosie del Seraglio, which he wrote in 1773 in
Milan for his "Lucio Silla. "


685   "Twelve o' Clock" [Midi]
      John Field.   Rondo in E  major for Piano  (Hopkinson
         13 K)

This was a revised version for Piano of his "Divertio
sement avec Quartet No. 1" [divertimento with quartet no.
1].


686   "L'Uccelliera"  (see "The Aviary")
      Luigi Boccherini.   Quintet No. 12 for Two Violins,
         Viola and Two Cellos in D major, op. 11 no. 6
         (Gérard 276)


687   "Det Udslukkelige"  (see "The Inextinguishable")
      Carl Nielsen.   Symphony No. 4


688   "Die Uhr"  (see "The Clock")
      Haydn.   Symphony No. 101 in D major  (Hob. I, 101)


689   "Uncertainty"
      Chopin.   Prelude, op. 28 no. 5, in D major  (Brown
         107, No. 5)

Each of the Op. 28 preludes of Chopin was given a subtitle by Hans von Bülow.   Of this one he said, "The alternating B and B flat indicate debate--'Yes' and 'No!'   Later
it grows more vacillating; the keys change from moment to
moment, until at the end it closes with an outburst of vexation and obstinacy" [Musician, xvi (1911)].


690   "Unfinished"
      Borodin.   Symphony No. 3 in A minor

Alexander Borodin wrote two movements of a third
symphony, a Moderato and a Scherzo.   These were orches-

trated by Glazounov and published posthumously as the "Unfinished."

691 "Unfinished"
Bruckner. Symphony No. 9 in D minor

When Bruckner died this symphony was incomplete. The first three movements were fully scored but Bruckner's sketches gave only a fragmentary idea of what he intended for the Finale. Many listeners feel that the serene close of the Adagio is the fitting and perfect ending for the symphony and that a finale in fact would be something of an anti-climax. Like Schubert's Eighth, Bruckner's Ninth seems complete in its incompleteness.

692 "Unfinished" (see "Swan Song")
Haydn. String Quartet, op. 103, in B♭ major (Hob. III, 83)

693 "Unfinished" ("Reliquié")
Schubert. Sonata for Piano No. 15 in C major (D. 840)

The C major Sonata, which Schubert wrote in 1825 and which is known by its nickname "Unfinished," is complete except for the conclusion of the main section in the Minuet and the end of the Rondo Finale. The first two movements of the Sonata are as perfect in themselves and as nearly related to each other as those of the so-called "Unfinished Symphony." Both Ernst Křenek (in 1921) and Walter Rehberg (in 1927) have attempted to complete the sonata.

694 "Unfinished"
Schubert. Symphony No. 8 in B minor (D. 759)

There has been great speculation as to why Schubert wrote only two movements for this B minor Symphony. Actually, he wrote nine measures of a third movement, a Scherzo, but quickly abandoned it. In all probability, Schubert realized that he had a complete artistic and emotional whole to which any additions would be objectionable. "Let us be thankful," says Philip Hale, "that Schubert never

finished the work.    Possibly the lost arms of the Venus de
Milo might disappoint if they were found and restored. "
         Another mystery is the unbelievably long delay be-
tween the writing of the Symphony in 1822 and the first performance on December 17, 1865, at a concert of the Society of Friends of Music in Vienna.    In Einstein's book,
Schubert, A Musical Portrait, there is the following:
         "Josef Hüttenbrenner, who gave the Viennese music-
director Herbeck the first information of the existence of
the manuscript in his brother Anselm's possession (8 April
1860) simply explained that Schubert gave it to him 'as a
present for Anselm, in token of his appreciation for having
sent him, through me, the Diploma of Honour of the Graz
Music Society. '  Anselm never delivered the manuscript,
but kept it himself.    In his biography of his father ...
Ludwig Herbeck has given us an interesting description of
how, on 30 April 1865, Johann Herbeck visited Ober-An-
dritz, near Graz, whither Anselm Hüttenbrenner had re-
tired.    There, in a drawer stuffed full of papers, he discovered the manuscript and rescued it from the suspicious
old man, a curious character who labored under the con-
viction that he was an unappreciated genius.    Since then it
has become one of the best known symphonic works in the
world" [pp. 202-03].


695   "Variation Symphony"
      Peter Mennin.   Symphony No. 7

      Mennin's seventh symphony is in a single movement but
it comprises five sections.   The composer explained that the
work, though subtitled "Variation Symphony," has little relationship to the consecutive variation principle but instead
uses techniques of variation resulting from over all structural and dramatic concept.


696   "Variations on an Old English Nursery Song" [A Frog
      He Went A-Courting]
      Hindemith.   Piece for Cello and Piano


697   "Variations Sérieuses"
      Corelli.   La Folia (Variations for Violin and Continuo)

      The name "La Folia" is originally that of a type of
Portugese dance made famous by Corelli's Variations.    Far

from being the solemn melody which modern violinists make
it and from which the subtitle, "Variations Sérieuses,"
stems, it was originally a noisy dance accompanied by tam-
bourines and performed by men dressed as women, who be-
haved so wildly that they appeared to be out of their senses.


698   "Venetian Boat Song" (named by composer)  (see "Songs
          Without Words")
      Mendelssohn.   Piece for Piano, op. 19 no. 6, in G
          minor


699   "Venetian Boat Song" (named by composer)  (see "Songs
          Without Words")
      Mendelssohn.   Piece for Piano, op. 30 no. 6, in F#
          minor


700   "Venetian Boat Song" (named by composer)  (see "Songs
          Without Words")
      Mendelssohn.   Piece for Piano, op. 62 no. 5, in A
          minor


701   "The Victory of Hero Koburg" [Der Sieg vom Helden
          Koburg]
      Mozart.   Contretanz for Small Orchestra   (K. 587)

      This piece quotes a march song in honor of the Austri-
an victory over the Turks on September 22, 1789, at Mar-
tinestie by General Friedrich Josias, Prince Koburg-Saalfeld.


702   "Victory Symphony"  (see "Fate Symphony")
      Beethoven.   Symphony No. 5, op. 67, in C minor


703   "Die vier Temperamente"  (see "The Four Tempera-
          ments")
      Carl Nielsen.   Symphony No. 2 in B minor


704   "Vision"
      Chopin.   Prelude, op. 28 no. 9, in E major   (Brown
          107, no. 9)

The following is one of Hans von Bülow's fancies as to
why he subtitled this prelude "Vision" (he gave subtitles to
all of Chopin's Op. 28 preludes).  The commentary is almost surrealistic:
      "Here Chopin has the conviction that he has lost his
power of invention.  With the determination to discover
whether his brain can still originate ideas he strikes his
head with a hammer (here the sixteenths and thirty-seconds
are to be carried out in exact time, indicating a double
stroke of the hammer).  In the third and fourth measures
one can hear the blood trickle (trills in the left hand).  He
is desperate at finding no inspiration (fifth measure); he
strikes again with the hammer and with greater force (thirty-
seconds twice in succession during the crescendo).  In the
key of A flat he finds his powers again; appeased, he seeks
his former key and closes contentedly" [Musician, xvi
(1911)].


705   "The Vision" (also, "Fleecy Cloud") (see "Songs With-
      out Words")
      Mendelssohn.  Piece for Piano, op. 53 no. 2, in E♭
      major


706   "Der Vogel" (see "The Bird")
      Haydn.  String Quartet, op. 33 no. 3, in C major
      (Russian Quartet) (Hob. III, 39)


707   "Der Wachtelschlag" (see "The Call of the Quail")
      Haydn.  No. 6 of a Set of Piano Pieces for Musical
      Clocks (Hob. XIX, 8)


708   "Wagner Symphony"
      Bruckner.  Symphony No. 3 in D minor

      This symphony is so called because it was dedicated
to Wagner by Bruckner.  The composer visited Wagner in
Bayreuth and showed him several works, asking permission
to dedicate one to him--this one (with the bold trumpet
theme) is the one Wagner preferred.


709   "Wait Till the Clouds Roll By"
      Haydn.  String Quartet, op. 77 no. 2, in F major
      (Hob. III, 82)

There is an old song in England called "Wait Till the Clouds Roll By" and it is because of the similarity between the opening phrase of the quartet and this song that the quartet has been so nicknamed.


710   "Waldstein"
      Beethoven.   Sonata for Piano, op. 53, in C major

The first, and in every way the most important, of Beethoven's patrons was Count Ferdinand Ernst Gabriel Waldstein.   He recognized the great genius of Beethoven and did everything in his power financially and spiritually to encourage it.
      Count Waldstein was also very musical and in 1791 or 1792 Beethoven wrote 12 variations for four hands on one of his themes.   When Beethoven dedicated the important Sonata Op. 53 to the Count it was only a proof of the gratitude which had lived on in the mature man.


711   "Wallenstein"
      Josef Rheinberger.   Symphony No. 1, op. 10


712   "The Wanderer" (see "Songs Without Words")
      Mendelssohn.   Piece for Piano, op. 30 no. 4, in B
      minor


713   "Der Wanderer"
      Schubert.   Fantasy for Piano, op. 15, in C major   (D.
      760)

In October 1816 one of Schubert's most famous songs was published as Op. 4, No. 1, under the title of "Der Wanderer." The song was so successful that Schubert used the first phrase, the one at the words:  "Die Sonne dünkt mich hier so kalt,/ Die Blüte welk, das Lebel alt" [here the sun seems to me so cold, The flowers faded and life's old] as the central point of his brilliant work.


714   "War Sonatas"
      Prokofiev.   Three sonatas for piano:   No. 6 in A
      major, op. 82; No. 7 in B♭ major, op. 83; No. 8
      in B♭ major, op. 84

Prokofiev himself called these three compositions, "War Sonatas. "


715   "The Water Music"
      Handel.   Suite for Orchestra in F major and D major

The traditional story of "The Water Music," although disputed, is as follows:  King George I and Handel were not on very good terms, and in order to bring about a reconciliation, two friends of Handel, Lord Burlington and Baron Kielmansegg, devised a scheme.   On the occasion of a royal water party on the Thames, it was arranged that the King's barge should be followed by another on which were Handel and a group of musicians.   The music that was played was a suite especially composed by Handel for this occasion.

The King liked the music and asked the name of the composer, and being told that it was Handel, immediately took him back into his favor, gave him £200 a year pension, and took him on a journey to Hanover in 1716.

Sir Newman Flower, in his well documented George Frideric Handel [p. 105], says the following about "The Water Music":  "The story is so ridden with romance that it is precisely what ought to have happened.   As a matter of fact, 'The Water Music' was not produced until 1717 and then under very different circumstances.   The document in the Berlin Archives recently disclosed is the report made by the Brandenburg envoy to the English Court, Frederic Bonnet, and is dated July 19, 1717.

"By the side of the Royal Barge was that of the musicians to the number of 50, who played all kinds of instruments, viz. trumpet, hunting horns, oboes, bassoons, German flutes, French flutes à bec, violins and basses. The concert was composed expressly for the occasion by the famous Handel, native of Halle, and first composer of the King's music.   It was so strongly approved by H. M. that he commanded it to be repeated, once before and once after supper, although it took an hour for each performance. "

There is no contemporary account of what the music actually included on this occasion and the composer's autograph manuscript seems lost.   It is quite possible that the composer's 25 separate numbers in the "Water Music," as we now know it, may represent Handel's share in numerous water parties.   Much research has been made to try to discover what actual music was played on that historic barge trip, but to no avail.

716   "Weber's Last Thought"
      K. C. Reissiger.  Danse Brillante, op. 26 no. 5, for
      Piano

      Percy Scholes [Oxford Companion, p. 654] has explained
that this piece had been thought to be one of Karl Maria von
Weber's but it has been proven to have been composed by
Reissiger.
      Reissiger played these dances for Weber in Febru-
ary 1826 just before Weber left for London.  For some reason Weber wanted a copy of this No. 5 and Reissiger wrote
it out for him immediately.  When Weber died in London
this was found among his possessions; as it was thought to
be his, it was published with the subtitle, "Weber's Last
Thought."  The error was revealed to Reissiger, the actual
composer of the music, when another composer J. B. Pixis
innocently sent him a copy of one of his own compositions,
called "Fantasia on Weber's Last Thought."


717   "Wedding Cake"
      Saint-Saëns.  Valse Caprice for Piano and Orchestra,
      op. 76

      This scintillating work was written in 1885.  It is a
chain of glittering waltzes which might have reminded Saint-
Saëns of a multilayer cake attractively iced and decorated
and most appropriate for a wedding.


718   "Wedding Cantata"
      J. S. Bach.  Vergnügte Pleissen Stadt--Cantata 216
      [Joyous Pleissen City] (BWV 216)

      This is a lately recovered cantata that Bach had com-
posed for the wedding banquet of the Leipzig merchant,
Heinrich Wolff, and the daughter of Hempel, the Commissar
of Excise in Zittau.
      The text is by Picander, who gives speaking parts
to the rivers "Pleisse" and "Neisse."  Bach scored it for
two voices, a soprano and an alto.  At a later date Bach
recast the text, substituting Apollo and Mercury for the
"Pleisse" and the "Neisse" and made them sing the praise
of Leipzig and its council.

719   "Wedding Cantata"
      J. S. Bach.   Dem Gerechten muss das Licht--Cantata
      195   (BWV 195)

It is believed that Bach wrote both the libretto and
music for this "Wedding Cantata" but we do not know for
whose wedding it was composed.   The indications are that
the music was written in a hurry.   First, because in place
of an Aria, Recitative and Chorus in the second part, there
is only a choral, and secondly because in the "Vor der
Trauung" section, music that Bach had composed for oth
er works is used again.

720   "Wedding Cantata"
      J. S. Bach.   Der Herr denket an uns--Cantata 196
      (BWV 196)

This "Wedding Cantata" was composed in June 1708
for the marriage of Regina Wiedemann, an aunt of Bach's
first wife, and Pastor Johann Lorenz Stauber.

721   "Wedding Cantata"
      J. S. Bach.   Weichet nur, betrübte Schatten--Cantata
      202   (BWV 202)

"Weichet nur, betrübte Schatten" is a specially delightful piece of music written for solo soprano and chamber orchestra.   We do not know the name of the couple for whose
wedding this was composed but it is very possible that Anna
Magdalena was the soprano who sang the part.   Actually the
cantata would have been lost had not Rinck, a pupil of Peter
Kellner, copied it out.

722   "Wedding Cantata"
      J. S. Bach.   O Holder Tag--Cantata 210   (BWV 210)

If the text of "O Holder Tag" can be trusted, the
couple for whom the "Wedding Cantata" was composed was
a musical one.   The question discussed was whether music
ought to have a place in a wedding feast.   The answer is
yes, particularly that this Cantata was written for "patrons"
of the art.
        As a special gift the couple each received a copy
of the parts which were written with extra neatness and

fastened with a silk ribbon.   These are now in the Royal
Library of Berlin.


723   "Wedge Fugue"
      J. S. Bach.   Fugue for Organ in E minor   (BWV 548)

      The subject of this fugue has a definite rocking motion
and works outward by contrary motion from a single note to
an octave.   The result suggests a "wedge" to the ear as
well as to the eye.   In Germany it is also known as "The
Scissors Fugue. "


724   "Die Weihe der Töne" (see "The Consecration of
      Sound")
      Louis Spohr.   Symphony No. 4, in F major, op. 86


725   "Die Weihe des Hauses"   (see "The Consecration of
      the House")
      Beethoven.   Overture, op. 124, in C major


726   "Weihnachtsoratorium" (see "Christmas Oratorio")
      J. S. Bach.   Six Church Cantatas   (BWV 248)


727   "Wellington's Victory" (see "The Battle of Vittoria")
      Beethoven.   Symphony for Orchestra, op. 91


728   "The White Mass"
      Scriabin.   Sonata No. 7, op. 53

      Faubion Bowers tells us that none of Scriabin's music
pleased him as much as his Seventh Sonata.   As his favorite
piece he played it repeatedly in concert and in private.   He
considered it "holy, " marked some passages "très pur"
(very pure), and thought its sonorities saintly.   He himself
subtitled the Sonata "The White Mass" to dramatize its
sacerdotal character and to him its performance was ritual.
[From Scriabin, v. II, p. 231. ]


729   "Wind Band Mass" [Harmoniemesse]
      Haydn.   Mass in B♭ major (Hob. XXII, 14)

The Mass in B♭ major written in 1802 is known by this
popular name because of the emphatic use of wind instruments.


730   "Winter Day Dreams" (also, "Winter Reveries")
      Tchaikovsky.   Symphony No. 1 in G minor

In the winter of 1866, Tchaikovsky was teaching at the
Moscow Conservatory.   Besides his 26 hours a week of
teaching, he was also composing, among other things, his
first symphony.   This work seemed to have caused him a
great deal of anguish and when in the summer of that year
he had sent it to Petersburg for criticism from his one-time
masters, Anton Rubinstein and Zaremba, the two sent it
back with many criticisms.   At first, Tchaikovsky accepted
the suggestions for the changes, but later he erased the al-
terations and the symphony had a first successful performance
in Moscow in the spring of the following year.
      It is probably because of the subtitle of the first
movement, "Winter Reverie on a Journey," that the nickname for the symphony originated.   James G. Huneker, the
famous critic, said of the opening movement, "The slush
must have been ankle deep. "


731   "The Winter Wind"
      Chopin.  Etude for Piano, op. 25 no. 11, in A minor
        (Brown 83)

This etude, which Chopin wrote in 1834, has been nicknamed "Winter Wind" because of the constant figuration in
the right hand which is supposed to depict the wind.   Herbert
Weinstock, in his book, Chopin, The Man and His Music,
has the following to say about it:
      "The nickname, however, must not be taken as an
excuse for misunderstanding the music as music.   Except
for the four measures of introduction (an after-thought on
Chopin's part) and the fourth and third measures from the
end, the melody is carried in the left hand while the right
hand supplies washes and fountainings of piano tone and
melodic color.   The last four measures are a master stroke
--a simple cadence followed by the melodic minor scale run
upwards in octaves over a range of twenty-nine notes.   This
extreme harmonic simplicity seems the only possible ending
for so richly harmonized a piece, but is exactly the sort of
fulfillment that it takes genius to discover" [p. 215].

732 "Witches Minuet" [Hexenmenuett]
Haydn. Minuet of String Quartet, op. 76 no. 2, in D
minor (Hob. III, 76)

This minuet is a strange piece, actually a canon, in
which the two violins play the melody in octaves, while viola
and cello (also in octaves) play the imitation. It is the octave doubling that gives the weird effect and the nickname.

733 "With Two Eyeglasses Obbligato" [Mit zwei obligaten
Augengläsern]
Beethoven. Duo for Viola and Cello in E♭ major
(WoO 32)

The title would suggest that the piece was meant for
two definite players to whose shortsightedness Beethoven
jocularly alluded with the remark, "Mit zwei obligaten Au-
gengläsern." The cellist was a friend of Beethoven named
Nikolaus von Zmeskall, and the composer himself played the
viola.
It was not until 1912 that Fritz Stein discovered the
piece in London and edited only the first movement for Pet-
ers of Leipzig. The second movement was published in
1952. The autograph is found in the so-called Kafka Sketch-
book, from the period 1784-1800, which was purchased by
the British Museum in 1875, and was recently edited by
Joseph Kerman.
The original score seems to have been written very
hurriedly and is hard to decipher. It contains very little but
the notes, dynamic directions are completely missing, and
bowing is indicated only in three bars. In Beethoven's hand-
writing is scribbled, "Duett Mit Zwei Obligaten Augenglä-
sern. "

734 "Without Repose" (see "Songs Without Words")
Mendelssohn. Piece for Piano, op. 30 no. 2, in B♭
minor

735 "Die Wut über den verlornen Groschen ausgetobt in
einer Caprice" (see "The Rage Over a Lost Penny")
Beethoven. Capriccio for Piano in G major, op. 129

736 "Year 1905"
Shostakovich. Symphony No. 11 in G minor

This symphony, popularly called "Year 1905," is the story of the 1905 Revolution. It is significantly full of Revolutionary songs. In his notes on the recording, Edward Tatnall Canby asks, "Is it not possible that perhaps unconsciously the G minor was to Shostakovich the key of the oppressed Russian people and the dissonant opposing tones of the half-step, the forces of Tzarist oppression?"

737  "Youth"
      Kabalovsky. Concerto trilogy: Concerto for Piano No. 3, op. 50; Concerto for Violin, op. 48; Concerto for Cello, op. 49

    The piano concerto is the last work of the trilogy and was composed in 1952. All three concertos have been subtitled "Youth" because of their youthful vitality and extreme melodic appeal.

738  "Z mého zivota" (see "From My Life")
      Bedřich Smetana. String Quartet No. 1 in E minor

739  "Les Zéphyrs"
      Chopin. Nocturnes for Piano, op. 15 (Brown 55, 79)

740  "Zlonické Zvony" (see "The Bells of Zlonice")
      Dvořák. Symphony No. 1 in C minor (Burghauser 9)

# BIBLIOGRAPHY

Abraham, Gerald. Borodin; The Composer and His Music.
London: W. Reeves [1927]

_____. Eight Soviet Composers. London: Oxford University Press, 1932.

_____, ed. The Music of Schubert. New York: W. W.
Norton [1947]

Anderson, Emily, ed. The Letters of Mozart and His Family. 3 vols. London: Macmillan, 1938.

Apthorp, William F. and J. D. Champlin. Cyclopedia of
Music and Musicians. New York: Scribner's, 1888-93.

Bacharach, A. L. British Music of Our Time. New York:
Penguin Books, 1946.

_____. Lives of the Great Composers. 2 vols. New
York: Penguin Books, 1947.

Bagar, Robert and Louis Biancolli. The Concert Companion.
New York: McGraw-Hill, 1947.

Baker's Biographical Dictionary of Musicians. 5th ed. Rev.
by Nicolas Slonimsky. New York: G. Schirmer, 1958-
71.

Bauer, Marion. 20th Century Music. New York: Putnam,
1933.

Bedford, Herbert. Robert Schumann; His Life and Work.
New York: Harper, 1925.

Behrend, Jeanne, ed. Piano Music by Louis Moreau Gottschalk. Bryn Mawr, Pa. : Theodore Presser, 1956.

181

Behrend, William.  Ludwig van Beethoven's Pianoforte Sonatas, tr. by Ingeborg Lund.  London:  J. M. Dent, 1927.

Bekker, Paul.  Beethoven, tr. by M. M. Bozman.  London: J. M. Dent, 1927.

Bertennson, Sergei and Jay Leyda.  Sergei Rachmaninoff; A Lifetime in Music.  New York:  New York University Press, 1956.

Blom, Eric.  Mozart.  New York:  Dutton, 1935.

Bowen, Catherine D. and Barbara von Meck.  "Beloved Friend"; The Story of Tchaikowsky and Nadejda von Meck. New York:  Random House, 1937.

Bowers, Faubion.  Scriabin.  2 vols.  Tokyo:  Kodansha [1969]

Brenet, Michel.  Haydn, tr. by Leonard Leese.  London: Oxford University Press, 1926.

Brown, Maurice J. E.  Chopin.  An Index of His Works in Chronological Order.  2d ed.  London:  Macmillan, 1972.

Bülow, Hans von.  "Chopin's Préludes, op. 28, analyzed," tr. by Frederick S. Law, Musician, xvi (1911), 88, 137-38.

Burghauser, Jarmil.  Antonín Dvořák.  Thematic Catalogue, Bibliography, Survey of His Life and Work.  Prague, 1967.

Burk, John N.  The Life and Works of Beethoven.  New York:  Random House, 1943.

_____.  Mozart and His Music.  New York:  Random House, 1943.

Burke, Cornelius G.  The Collector's Haydn.  Philadelphia: Lippincott, 1959.

Cauchie, Maurice.  Thematic Index of the Works of François Couperin.  Monaco:  Lyrebird Press, 1949.

Clough, Francis F. and G. J. Cuming.  The World's Encyclopedia of Recorded Music.  London:  Sidgwick & Jackson, 1952-57.

Cobbett, Walter Wilson.  Cyclopedic Survey of Chamber
Music.  2d ed.  3 vols.  London:  Oxford University
Press, 1963.

Cross, Milton and David Ewen.  Encyclopedia of the Great
Composers and Their Music.  New York:  Doubleday,
1935.

Crowest, Frederick J.  A Book of Musical Anecdotes.  2
vols  London;  R. Bentley & Son, 1878.

Cudworth, Charles.  'Ye Old Spuriosity Shop,' Notes, xii
(1954-55), 25, 40, 533-35.

Culshaw, John.  Sergei Rachmaninov.  London:  Dennis
Dobson, 1949.

Cummings, William Henry.  Henry Purcell, 1658-1695.
New York:  Scribner's, 1911.

Deutsch, Otto Erich.  The Schubert Reader.  New York:
W. W. Norton, 1947.

_____.  Schubert; Memoirs by His Friends, tr. by Rosa-
mond Levy.  New York:  Macmillan, 1958.

_____.  Handel; A Documentary Biography.  New York:
W. W. Norton [1955]

_____.  Schubert; Thematic Catalogue of All His Works.
London:  J. M. Dent, 1951.

Doernberg, Erwin.  The Life and Symphonies of Anton
Bruckner.  London:  Barrie and Rockliff, 1960.

Drinker, Henry S., Jr.  The Chamber Music of Brahms.
Philadelphia:  Elkan-Vogel, 1932.

Einstein, Alfred.  Schubert; A Musical Portrait.  New York:
Oxford University Press, 1951.

_____.  Mozart; His Character, His Work.  New York:
Oxford University Press, 1945.

_____.  Music in the Romantic Era.  New York:  W. W.
Norton, 1947.

Engel, Gabriel.  The Symphonies of Anton Bruckner.  New York:  Bruckner Society, 1955.

Erskine, John.  Song Without Words; The Story of Felix Mendelssohn.  New York:  Julian Messner, 1941.

Evans, Edwin.  Handbook to the Chamber and Orchestral Works of Johannes Brahms.  2 vols.  New York:  Scribner's [1933-35]

_____.  Handbook to the Pianoforte Works of Johannes Brahms.  New York:  Scribner's [1936]

_____.  Handbook to the Vocal Works of Brahms.  New York:  Scribner's, 1912.

Ewen, David.  The Complete Book of Twentieth Century Music.  Englewood Cliffs, N. J.:  Prentice Hall [1968]

Flower, Sir Newman.  George Frideric Handel; His Personality and Times.  New York:  Scribner's, 1948.

Forkel, Johann Nikolaus.  Johann Sebastian Bach.  London:  Constable, 1920.

Foss, Hubert J.  Ralph Vaughan Williams.  New York:  Oxford University Press, 1950.

_____, ed.  The Heritage of Music.  3 vols.  London:  Oxford University Press, 1927-51.

Friskin, James and Irwin Freundlich.  Music for the Piano.  New York:  Rinehart [1954]

Fuld, James J.  The Book of World-Famous Music.  New York:  Crown Publishers [1966]

Geiringer, Karl.  Brahms; His Life and Works.  London:  G. Allen, 1936.

_____.  Haydn; A Creative Life in Music.  New York:  W. W. Norton, 1946.

Gérard, Yves.  Thematic, Bibliographical and Critical Catalogue of the Works of Luigi Boccherini.  London:  Oxford University Press, 1969.

Gilman, Lawrence.  Edward MacDowell.  New York:  John
Lane, 1908.

_____.  Stories of Symphonic Music.  New York:  Harper
Bros., 1907.

Grace, Harvey.  The Organ Works of Bach.  London:  Novello & Co., 1922.

Griesinger, Georg August.  Biographische Notizen über
Joseph Haydn.  Leipzig:  Breitkopf & Härtel, 1810

Grove, Sir George, ed.  Grove's Dictionary of Music and
Musicians.  5th ed.  Rev. by Eric Blom.  9 vols.
and supple.  London:  Macmillan, 1954-61.

Hartog, Howard.  European Music in the Twentieth Century.
London:  Routledge and Kegan Paul [1957]

Hensel, Sebastian.  The Mendelssohn Family.  2 vols.  New
York:  Harper & Bros., 1882.

Hervey, Arthur.  Saint-Saëns.  New York:  Dodd, Mead,
1922.

Hoboken, Anthony van.  Joseph Haydn:  Thematisch-bibliographisches Werkverzeichnis.  Mainz:  B. Schotts Söhne,
1957-  .

Hoffmeister, Karel.  Antonín Dvořák.  London:  John Lane
[1928]

Holbrooke, Joseph.  Contemporary British Composers.  London:  Cecil Palmer [1925]

Hopkinson, Cecil.  A Bibliographical Thematic Catalogue of
the Works of John Field.  London, 1961.

Hughes, Gervase.  Dvořák; His Life and Music.  London:
Cassell, 1967.

Hughes, Rosemary.  Haydn.  London:  J. M. Dent, 1950.

Hull, A. Eaglefield.  Bach's Organ Works.  London:  Musical Opinion, 1929.

Huneker, James G.  Chopin; The Man and His Music.  New
York:  Scribner's, 1900.

_____. Franz Liszt. New York: Scribner's, 1911.

_____. Mezzotints in Modern Music. New York: Scribner's, 1899.

Hutcheson, Ernest. The Literature of the Piano. New York: Knopf, 1948.

Istituto Italiano Antonio Vivaldi. Antonio Vivaldi; Catalogo Numerico-Tematico delle Opere Strumentali. Milan: Ricordi, 1968.

Kalischer, A. C., ed. Beethoven's Letters. London: J. M. Dent, 1926.

Kelley, Edgar Stillman. Chopin, the Composer. New York: G. Schirmer, 1913.

Kinsky, Georg. Das Werk Beethovens. Thematisch-bibliographisches Verzeichnis seiner sämtlichen vollendeten Kompositionen. Munich: G. Henle, 1955.

Kirkpatrick, Ralph. Domenico Scarlatti. Princeton, N. J.: Princeton University Press, 1953.

Köchel, Ludwig, Ritter von. Chronologisch-thematisches Verzeichnis sämtlicher Tonwerke Wolfgang Amadé Mozarts. 6th ed. Wiesbaden: Breitkopf & Härtel [1964]

Krehbiel, Henry E. The Pianoforte and Its Music. New York: Scribner's, 1911.

Landon, H. C. Robbins, ed. The Mozart Companion. New York: W. W. Norton, 1956.

_____. "The Jena Symphony," Music Review, 18 (1957), 109-13.

_____. The Symphonies of Joseph Haydn. New York: Macmillan, 1956.

Lee, E. Markham. Brahms; The Man and His Music. London: Sampson, Low, Marston, 1916.

Litzmann, Berthold, ed. Letters of Clara Schumann and Johannes Brahms. 2 vols. London: Arnold, 1927.

Longo, Alessandro, ed. Domenico Scarlatti; Opere Complete per Clavicembalo. 10 vols., supple., thematic index. Milan: Ricordi, 1947-51.

Lyle, Watson. Camille Saint-Saëns; His Life and Art. London: Kegan Paul, 1923.

Mason, Daniel Gregory. The Chamber Music of Brahms. New York: Macmillan, 1933.

Mellers, Wilfrid H. François Couperin and the French Classical Tradition. New York: Roy [1951]

Mies, Paul. Volkstümliche Namen musikalischer Werke. Bonn: Musikhandel-Verlag [1960]

Murdoch, William. Brahms. London: Rich and Cowan, 1933.

_____. Chopin; His Life. London: Murray, 1934.

Nestyev, Israel V. Serge Prokofiev. New York: Knopf, 1946.

Nettl, Paul. The Book of Musical Documents. New York: Philosophical Library, 1948.

Newlin, Dika. Bruckner, Mahler, Schoenberg. New York: King's Crown Press, 1947.

Niecks, Frederick. Frederic Chopin as a Man and Musician. London: Novello, 1902.

_____. Robert Schumann. London: J. M. Dent, 1925.

Niemann, Walter. Brahms. New York: Knopf, 1920.

Nottebohm, Gustav. Beethoveniana; Aufsätze und Mittheilungen. Leipzig: J. Rieter-Biedermann, 1872.

Offergeld, Robert. The Centennial Catalogue of the Published and Unpublished Compositions of Louis Moreau Gottschalk. New York: Stereo Review, 1970.

Pakenham, Simona. Ralph Vaughan Williams. London: Macmillan, 1957.

Parry, Sir Hubert H.   Johann Sebastian Bach.   New York:
G. P. Putnam's, 1909.

Pincherle, Marc.   Corelli; His Life, His Work.   New York:
W. W. Norton, 1956.

_____.  Vivaldi, Genius of the Baroque.   New York: W.
W. Norton, 1957.

Prod'homme, Jacques G.   La Jeunesse de Beethoven (1770-
1800).   Paris:  Payot, 1921.

Radcliffe, Philip.   Mendelssohn.   London:  J. M. Dent,
1954.

Ramann, Lina.   Franz Liszt, Artist and Man.   London:
W. H. Allen, 1882.

Rayson, Ethel.   Polish Music and Chopin, Its Laureate.
London:  W. Reeves, 1916.

Redlich, Hans F.   Bruckner and Mahler.   New York:  Far-
rar, Strauss & Cudahy, 1963.

Rubinstein, Anton.   Autobiography, tr. by Aline Delano.
Boston:  Little, Brown, 1903.

Saint-Saëns, Camille.   Musical Memories.   Boston:  Small,
Maynard, 1919.

Schauffler, Robert Haven.   Beethoven; The Man Who Freed
Music.   New York:  Doubleday, Doran, 1929.

Schmieder, Wolfgang.   Thematisches-systematisches Verzeichnis der musikalischen Werke von Johann Sebastian
Bach.   Leipzig:  Breitkopf & Härtel, 1950.

Scholes, Percy.   The Oxford Companion to Music.   10th ed.
London:  Oxford University Press, 1970.

Schonberg, Harold C.   The Great Pianists.   New York:
Simon & Schuster, 1963.

Schumann, Robert.   On Music and Musicians.   New York:
Pantheon, 1947.

Schweitzer, Albert.   J. S. Bach, tr. by Ernest Newman.
2 vols.   New York:  Dover Publishers, 1966.

Seaman, Julian, ed.   Great Orchestral Music; A Treasury
of Program Notes.   New York:  Rinehart, 1950.

Seroff, Victor I.   Dmitri Shostakovich; The Life and Background of a Soviet Composer.   New York:  Knopf, 1943.

Sitwell, Sacheverell.   Liszt.   London:  Faber & Faber,
1934.

Slonimsky, Nicolas.   Music Since 1900.   4th ed.   New York:
Scribner's, [1971]

_____, ed.   The International Cyclopedia of Music and
Musicians.   9th ed.   New York:  Dodd, Mead, 1964.

Somfai, Laszlo.   "Zur Echtheitsfrage des Haydn'schen 'Opus
3'," Haydn Jahrbuch, 3 (1965), 153-63.

Sourek, Otakar.   Antonín Dvořák; His Life and Works.   New
York:  Philosophical Library, 1954.

Specht, Richard.   Johannes Brahms, tr. Eric Blom.   London:  J. M. Dent, [1930]

Spitta, Philipp.   Johann Sebastian Bach, tr. by Clara Bell
and J. A. Fuller Maitland.   2 vols.   London:  Novello,
1899.

Spohr, Louis.   Autobiography.   London:  Longman's, Green,
1865.

Stefan, Paul.   Antonín Dvořák.   New York:  Greystone
Press, 1941.

Stratton, Stephen S.   Niccolò Paganini.   New York:  Scribner's, 1917.

Terry, Charles Sanford.   Bach; A Biography.   London:  Oxford University Press, 1928.

_____.  Bach; The Cantatas and Oratorios.   London:  Ox-
ford University Press, 1925.

_____.  The Music of Bach.   London:  Oxford University
Press, 1933.

Thayer, Alexander W.   Thayer's Life of Beethoven, rev.

and ed. by Elliot Forbes.   Princeton, N. J. :   Princeton
University Press, 1967.

Tovey, Sir Donald F.   Beethoven.   London:  Oxford University Press, 1944.

_____.  A Companion to Beethoven's Pianoforte Sonatas.
London:  Associated Board of the Royal School of Music,
1935.

_____.  Essays in Musical Analysis.   6 vols.   London:
Oxford University Press, 1935-39.

Townsend, Pauline D.   Joseph Haydn.   New York: Scribner's, 1915.

Turner, Walter J.   Mozart; The Man and His Works.   New
York:  Knopf, 1938.

Tyson, Alan and H. C. R. Landon.   "Who Composed Haydn's
Op. 3?"  Musical Times, 105 (1964), 506-7.

Ulrich, Homer.   Chamber Music.   New York:  Columbia
University Press, 1948.

Vogel, J. P.   "Die 'Grazer Fantasie' von Franz Schubert,"
Die Musikforschung, 24 (1971), 168-72.

Walter, Bruno.   Gustav Mahler, tr. by James Galston.
London:  Kegan Paul, 1937.

Weinstock, Herbert.   Chopin; The Man and His Music.   New
York:  Knopf, 1949.

_____.  Handel.   New York:  Knopf, 1946.

_____.  Tchaikovsky.   London:  Cassell, 1946.

Williams, Charles Francis Abdy.   Handel.   London:  J. M.
Dent, 1935.

Young, Percy M.   Sir Edward Elgar:  A Study of a Musician.   London:  Collins, 1955.

Zimmerman, Franklin B.   Henry Purcell, 1659-1695; An
Analytic Catalogue of His Music.   London:  Macmillan,
1963.

# COMPOSER INDEX

(the numbers after each composition refer to serial entry numbers)

ARNE, THOMAS AUGUSTINE,
1710-1778
A Maggot 399
Organ concerto no. 3 399

BACH, CARL PHILIPP
EMANUEL, 1714-1788
Hamburger Sonate 275

BACH, JOHANN CHRISTIAN,
1735-1782
La Céleste 81
Lucio Silla 396
Symphony in B♭ (op. 18
no. 2) 396
Symphony in E♭ (op. 9
no. 2) 81

BACH, JOHANN SEBASTIAN,
1685-1750
Air on the G string 11
Aria with Thirty Variations
242
Bauern-Cantate 487
Brandenburg Concertos 57
Cantata no. 195 Wedding
719
Cantata no. 196 Wedding
720
Cantata no. 198 Funeral
Ode 224
Cantata no. 201 Phoebus
and Pan 490
Cantata no. 202 Wedding
721
Cantata no. 210 Wedding
722
Cantata no. 211 Coffee 101
Cantata no. 212 Peasant 487

Cantata no. 216 Wedding 718
Capriccio (BWV 992) 459
Christmas Oratorio 95
Coffee Cantata 101
Concerto, Italian 327
Concertos (Brandenburg) 57
Corelli Fugue 110
Dorian 148
English Suites 173
Fantasie & Fugue (BWV 542)
256
Fiddle Fugue 198
French Suites 209
Fugue (Corelli) 110
Fugue (Fiddle) 198
Fugue (Giant) 238
Fugue (Jig) 337
Fugue (Little) 377
Fugue (St. Anne) 559
Fugue (Scissors) 723
Fugue (Short) 581
Fugue (Wedge) 723
Funeral Ode 224
German Suites 234
Giant Fugue 238
Goldberg Variations 242
Great Fugue 256
Italian Concerto 327
Jig Fugue 337
Kaffee-Cantate 101
Little Fugue 377
On the Departure of a Beloved
Brother 459
Peasant Cantata 487
Phoebus and Pan 490
St. Anne's Fugue 559
Short G minor Fugue 581
Sopra la lontananza d'un fra-
tello diletto 459

191

# tan